D0416291

918349

The Fast-Track MBA Series

Co-published with PricewaterhouseCoopers

Consultant Editors
John Kind, Director, Human Resource Consulting,
PricewaterhouseCoopers
David Megginson, Associate Head, Sheffield Business School

THE FAST-TRACK MBA SERIES represents an innovative and refreshingly different approach to presenting core subjects in a typical MBA syllabus. The practical, action-oriented style is intended to involve the reader in self-assessment and participation.

Ideal for managers wanting to renew or develop their management capabilities, the books in THE FAST-TRACK MBA SERIES rapidly give readers a sound knowledge of all aspects of business and management that will boost both self-confidence and career prospects whether they have time to take an MBA or not. For those fortunate enough to take an MBA, the Series will provide a solid grounding in the subjects to be studied.

Managers and students worldwide will find this series an exciting and challenging alternative to the usual study texts and management guides.

Titles already available in this series are:

- *Strategic Management* (Robert Grant & James Craig)
- *Problem Solving and Decision Making* (Graham Wilson)
- *Human Resource Management* (Barry Cushway)
- *Macroeconomics* (Keith Wade & Francis Breedon)
- *Innovation and Creativity* (Jonne Ceserani & Peter Greatwood)
- *Leadership* (Philip Sadler)
- *Ethics in Organizations* (David J Murray)
- *Human Resource Development* (David Megginson, Jennifer Joy-Matthews & Paul Banfield)
- *Organizational Behavior and Design,* second edition (Barry Cushway & Derek Lodge)
- *Operations Management* (Donald Waters)

The Series Editors

John Kind is a director in the human resource consulting practice of PricewaterhouseCoopers and specializes in management training. He has wide experience of designing and presenting business education programmes in various parts of the world for clients such as BAA, Bass British Petroleum, DHL and Scottish Amicable Life Assurance Society He is a visiting lecturer at Henley Management College and holds an MBA from the Manchester Business School and an honours degree in Economics from the University of Lancaster.

David Megginson is a writer and researcher on self-development and the manager as developer. He has written *A Manager's Guide to Coaching, Self-development: A Facilitator's Guide, Mentoring in Action, Human Resource Development* in the Fast-track MBA series, *The Line Manager as Developer* and *Learning for Success*. He consults and researches in blue chip companies, and public and voluntary organizations. He is chairman of the European Mentoring Centre and an elected Council member of AMED, and has been Associate Head of Sheffield Business School and a National Assessor for the National Training Awards.

PricewaterhouseCoopers is a leading provider of professional services, including accountancy and audit, tax and management consultancy. It is the world's largest professional services practice.

THE *FAST-TRACK* (MBA) SERIES

ACCOUNTING
and
FINANCE *for Managers*

JOHN KIND

Published in association with
PriceWaterhouseCoopers

KOGAN
PAGE

DEDICATION

In memory of Michael Davies.

First published 1999

Kogan Page Limited
120 Pentonville Road
London
N1 9JN
UK

Kogan Page Limited
163 Central Avenue, Suite 4
Dover
NH 03820
USA

British Library Cataloguing in Publication Data

A CIP record for this book is available from the British Library.

ISBN 0 7494 2891 0

Typeset by Saxon Graphics Ltd, Derby
Printed and bound in Great Britain by Clays Ltd, St Ives plc

Contents

Acknowledgements

I wish to thank the following organizations for permission to reproduce information from their annual reports and other publications: BAA, BP, Coca-Cola, Datastream, *The Economist*, *The Financial Times*, Marks & Spencer, J Sainsbury, *The Sunday Times* and Unilever. Sara Arnold of Secret Genius in Winchester has done most of the hard work by typing the manuscript. Sara, thanks a million!

I am extremely grateful to Graham Mott, the author of the first edition, and all the executives for whom I have presented financial training programmes during the past 15 years. Without their inspiration, this book would not have been written.

John Kind

Introduction

The purpose of this book is to provide a straightforward but thorough introduction to accounting and finance for executives and managers who are studying these subjects, formally, for the first time. It is an entry-level text to be used before moving on to more advanced material.

A high degree of practicality and relevance are introduced with a strong 'real world' flavour supported by examples from leading international companies. The glossary of terms is designed to be as comprehensive as possible so that readers can obtain clear guidance at a time when they most need it.

The book is arranged in four parts. The first, 'The Financial Reporting Environment and an Introduction to Financial Statements', sets the external context within which financial statements are prepared and explains their meaning and significance.

The second part, 'Financial Statements in More Detail', looks at the published reports of Unilever. It provides an in-depth review of profit and loss accounts, balance sheets and cash flow statements using real-life examples from a major international business.

The third part, 'Financial Analysis', concentrates on the use of financial indicators to assess both the strengths and weaknesses of a business and to gain an insight into how financial performance might be improved.

The fourth part, 'Management Accounting', covers the use of management information for decision-making purposes, as well as budgetary control and investment appraisal (the financial evaluation of capital investment projects).

PART I

The Financial Reporting Environment and an Introduction to Financial Statements

CHAPTER 1

Financial Reporting

INTRODUCTION

As long ago as 1975, the Corporate Report, a discussion paper published by the Accounting Standards Committee reviewing how and to whom financial information should be presented, identified a number of user groups or stakeholders with whom an organization needs to interact. Although the list of interested parties has not changed, the detail and scope of the financial information they require has increased enormously. An audit report to shareholders, for example, is now at least 250 words long. Five years ago, 25 words would have sufficed!

STAKEHOLDERS

The stakeholders mentioned by the Corporate Report are:

- Shareholders – existing and potential investors need information to help them to decide whether to hold, buy or sell shares in a company.
- Lenders – both existing and potential lenders need to assess the risks involved – the possibility of default. They will be concerned to judge the ability of the borrower to service interest charges and to repay current and future amounts outstanding.
- Employees – individuals and their representatives need financial information to assess job security and job prospects and to support collective bargaining negotiations.

- Investment analysts and professional advisers – the financial press, 'the City' and financial advisers need access to and need to be able to understand financial information to advise their readers and clients.
- Business partners – suppliers, customers and competitors are all interested in an organization's financial performance, its reputation and its future prospects.
- Government – in addition to the possibility of the government being a customer or a creditor (a person or an organization to whom a business has a commitment), the taxation of profits requires the disclosure of certain financial information.
- The general public – information supplied, for example, to shareholders and business partners helps to inform employment and wealth creation issues.

Given the diverse needs of these various stakeholder groups, we need to take a brief look at the current regulatory framework.

THE REGULATORY FRAMEWORK

The accounting framework in the UK, as in other countries such as the United States, is becoming increasingly regulated. In the UK, these requirements are contained in:

- Companies Acts.
- Financial reporting standards (FRSs).
- Corporate governance reports.
- The Stock Exchange Listing Rules (rules applying to 'listed' companies – those whose shares are quoted on the London Stock Exchange).
- International Accounting Standards.
- Generally Accepted Accounting Principles (GAAP).

Companies Acts

The 1985 Companies Act states that financial statements must show a 'true and fair' view. It also states that five accounting concepts underlie their preparation; these are:

- going concern;
- consistency;
- prudence;
- accruals; and
- the separate valuation of assets and liabilities.

They will be explained in more detail in later chapters.

The 1989 Companies Act introduced a new requirement. Companies now have to state whether the financial statements have been prepared according to the relevant accounting standards and details have to be given of any variations from the standards and the reasons for them.

The 1985 Act consolidated much previous legislation and it was amended by the 1989 Act which contained most of the requirements to bring the UK into line with European Union practice.

Financial reporting standards

In November 1987, the CCAB (the Consultative Committee of Accountancy Bodies) appointed a review committee led by Sir Ron Dearing to recommend changes to the accounting standard-setting process. This was in the light of various accounting 'manoeuvres' which some companies had adopted to evade the rules.

In September 1988, the committee recommended that accounting standards should be issued by a new, totally independent body to be called the Accounting Standards Board (ASB). It was to supersede the Accounting Standards Committee which had issued standard statements of accounting practice (SSAPs) on topics such as accounting for stocks and VAT.

The Financial Reporting Council was also created to provide guidance to the new Accounting Standards Board on the appropriate priorities. The Dearing committee recommended the setting up of a Review Panel as well, to look at contentious departures from accounting standards by large companies.

The Accounting Standards Board, the Financial Reporting Council, and the Review Panel were set up in 1990. The Accounting Standards Board goes through a wide consultative process and issues exposure drafts called FREDs! These are Financial Reporting Exposure Drafts. They come out before financial reporting standards are issued. By October 1998, 14 financial reporting standards had been issued. The subjects range from cash flow statements, through acquisitions and mergers, to associated companies and joint ventures.

To improve the promptness of its response to important issues, a committee was set up: the Urgent Issues Task Force. Its purpose is to consider areas where an accounting standard or a Companies Act provision exists, but where unsatisfactory or conflicting interpretations have developed or are expected to develop in the future. The disclosure of directors' share options is an example.

The current UK accounting standard-setting system is summarized in Figure 1.1.

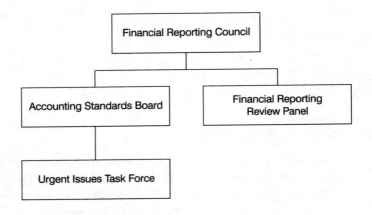

Figure 1.1   *The UK accounting standard-setting system*

The comparable body to the Accounting Standards Board in the United States is the Financial Accounting Standards Board, set up in 1973. There are now over 130 US accounting standards!

Internationally, the International Accounting Standards Committee produced its framework for the preparation and presentation of financial statements in 1989. The International Accounting Standards Committee itself was set up in 1973. Its members are drawn from professional bodies throughout the world. There are more than 100 of them from more than 80 countries and it issues its own accounting standards.

Corporate governance reports

This is an extremely fashionable subject and in the UK three reports have been issued since 1992. These are:

- The report of the Committee on the financial aspects of Corporate Governance; the code of best practice (the Cadbury Code). This was published in December 1992.
- Directors' remuneration – the Greenbury Committee Report which was issued in July 1995.
- The Committee on Corporate Governance – the final report of the Hampel Committee which came out in January 1998.

In July 1998, the Committee on Corporate Governance issued the 'combined code'. This new code consolidates the work of the three earlier committees. Listed companies now have to report on how they have applied the principles in the combined code. This means that the following matters need to be presented:

- details of the directors and their remuneration;
- relations with shareholders;
- accountability and audit matters which cover financial reporting, internal control, the Audit Committee and relationships with the external auditors.

The role of auditors

External auditors, such as PricewaterhouseCoopers, express an independent, professional opinion about the 'truth and fairness' of the financial statements. They express this opinion to shareholders who are responsible for appointing them. It is the responsibility of the directors to prepare these statements according to the requirements both of the Companies Acts and the relevant accounting standards. The auditors do *not* certify the financial statements as being right or wrong.

Here is an extract from the audit report of Marks & Spencer for the year ended 31 March 1998:

> In our opinion, the financial statements give a true and fair view of the state of affairs of the group at 31 March 1998 . . . they have been properly prepared in accordance with the Companies Act 1985.

Generally Accepted Accounting Principles (GAAP)

In the UK, the mandatory elements of GAAP are the 1985 Companies Act, Accounting Standards, abstracts issued by the Accounting Standard Board's Urgent Issues Task Force and, for listed companies, the Stock Exchange's Listing Rules. There are aspects of UK GAAP that relate to specific sectors such as the accounting requirements contained in legislation for banks and charities. There are also statements of recommended practice that are not mandatory. They are issued by organizations such as the Oil Industry Accounting Committee and the Association of British Insurers.

What is the practical effect of all these developments? The cynics would say 'A great deal of paper'! For example, the latest (1998) Marks & Spencer Annual Report contains:

- Chairman's Statement;
- Financial Review;
- Corporate Governance Report;
- the Audit Report;
- the Directors' Report.

All of this takes up 46 pages, quite apart from the 24 pages of financial statements and supporting notes.

SUMMARY

The regulatory environment is a good deal more complicated than it used to be. In the UK, the Companies Acts and the role of the Accounting Standards Board, through the issue of Financial Reporting Standards, are particularly important. Corporate governance is receiving a good deal of attention too following the publication of the Cadbury, Greenbury and Hampel reports since 1992.

The role of the external auditors is to provide an independent professional opinion to shareholders about the 'truth and fairness' of the financial statements prepared by the directors.

CHAPTER 2

An Introduction to the Profit and Loss Account

DEFINITION

The profit and loss account is concerned with measuring the financial performance of a business during a specified time period. 'Financial performance' in this context refers to one question and to one question only: 'Is the business profitable?'

Profit is the difference between the revenues or sales or turnover (these words have the same meaning) and the costs incurred in producing those revenues. Revenues represent the invoiced value of the goods and services provided to customers. Costs are the expenses involved in generating the revenues.

The practical application of the accounting convention of 'accruals' means that revenues are recognized at the time when the goods or services are provided and a sales invoice is raised. It is not when cash is received from customers. Similarly, costs are included in the profit and loss account according to the time period to which they relate and not when they are paid out in cash. Therefore, it is a serious misconception to think that the profit and loss account is a summary of the cash coming into and being paid out of a business. As a consequence, earning a profit and generating cash are not at all the same thing!

For example, in the year ended 31 March 1998, BAA, the airport operators, earned a profit after taxation (and all other costs) of £277 million. By contrast, its cash balances actually fell by £209 million, from £306 million to £97 million.

EXAMPLE

Take a look at Michael Owen Limited, which manufactures and markets T-shirts.

For the year ended 31 July 1998, it delivered goods to customers worth £5 million, both cash and on credit. The cash received from customers was £4 million. The cost of the T-shirts sold was £2.8 million, of which £2 million had been paid in cash. The balance outstanding to suppliers was, therefore, £800,000. All the T-shirts purchased from suppliers were sold. The other costs were:

Salaries for the year: £200,000.
Rent and business rates: £200,000, paid in cash, including rates of £40,000 for the six months ending 31 October 1998.
Advertising fees: £280,000 paid in cash. An invoice dated 15 July 1998 for £70,000 had not been paid.

What is Michael Owen Limited's profit for the year to 31 July 1998? Answer:

	£m
Revenues	5.00
Cost of products sold	(2.80)
Gross profit	2.20
Operating costs:	
Advertising	(0.35)
Salaries	(0.20)
Rent and rates	(0.18)
	(0.73)
Operating profit	**1.47**

Notes

Revenue equals the value of the products delivered and invoiced to customers. This is £5 million. The cash receipts of £4 million from customers are not relevant to the profit and loss account and should be ignored.

The cost of the T-shirts sold or the 'cost of sales' was £2.8 million. The difference between revenues and the cost of sales is the gross profit. In this case, it was £2.2 million. Gross profit is worked out before the deduction of business or operating costs such as advertising and salaries.

The salary cost is the cash paid out of £200,000.

The advertising cost is the cash paid out of £280,000 plus the unpaid invoice of £70,000, giving £350,000. The £70,000 is referred to as an accrual or an accrued charge. It is added to the cash payment of £280,000 to arrive at the advertising cost incurred during the financial year.

The cost of rent and business rates is £180,000. This is equal to the cash paid of £200,000 less £20,000 (a half of £40,000). Half of the £40,000 paid for business rates applies to the three months after the end of the financial year. It should be excluded, therefore, from the period whose profit and loss account we are preparing. The £20,000 paid in advance is called a pre-payment.

The profit of £1.47 million for the 12 months to the end of July 1998 is the operating or trading profit. It is the profit before any interest charges and taxation. They are not relevant in the case of Michael Owen, but they will be later!

CHAPTER 3

An Introduction to the Balance Sheet

DEFINITION

Whereas the profit and loss account is concerned with financial performance over a period of time, a balance sheet is concerned with the financial position of a business at a particular date. 'Financial position' means a summary of what the business *owns*, called 'assets', such as buildings, machinery and raw materials and what the business *owes*, called 'liabilities', such as amounts due to banks and amounts owing to suppliers. Thus a balance sheet is a financial photograph of a business at a particular date such as the end of the month or the end of the financial year.

A balance sheet is an example of the dual aspect, another important accounting convention. This stipulates that every accounting transaction has two equal and opposite elements. It is explained below and in Appendix B. Since these two elements must balance, total assets must always equal total liabilities. We need to know what the assets of a company are and how they have been financed. Details of the assets only provide an incomplete picture. We need to assess if they have been financed in a sensible way, for instance by not placing too much reliance on bank borrowings.

EXAMPLE

Michael Owen Limited set up in business on 1 August 1997. Michael contributed £500,000 of his own cash. At that stage, his balance sheet was:

1 August 1997
Assets   =   *Liabilities*
Cash   =   Issued share capital
£500,000   =   £500,000

Share capital is the permanent capital contributed by the owner or owners of a business both at the start of trading and, subsequently, when additional capital is required to finance expansion. Issued share capital is the amount of capital contributed in cash by a shareholder(s) and received by the business.

If some of the cash is spent to purchase a small office building (£80,000) and some office equipment (£20,000), there is no change in the balance sheet totals. However, there is a change in the nature of the assets since one asset, cash, has been exchanged for two different assets: an office building and office equipment.

Imagine that these transactions took place during the first week of August 1997. The balance sheet at 8 August 1997 will, therefore, be as follows:

Assets		*Liabilities*	
Office building	£80,000	Issued share capital	£500,000
Office equipment	£20,000		
Cash	£400,000		
	£500,000		**£500,000**

We know also that Michael Owen traded during the year to the end of July 1998. Therefore, we need to know what his balance sheet looked like at that date.

Assets (what the company owns)

Office building: £100,000.

Amounts due from customers – called trade debtors. We know that cash and credit sales total £5 million. We know also that the cash actually received from customers was £4 million. Therefore the amount still due from customers is £5 million less £4 million which is, of course, £1 million.

The company paid business rates of £40,000 for the six months to the end of October 1998. Therefore £20,000 applies to the period after 31 July 1998. This is called a pre-payment and is treated as an asset.

The remaining asset of the company is cash. We need to calculate the cash balance at the end of July 1998. This is equal to the cash balance at the start of the financial year plus cash receipts from whatever source, less cash payments for whatever purpose. There is no accounting sophistication involved here. It is simply a matter of accurate arithmetic.

Cash in	£m
Opening cash balance	0.50
Receipts from customers	4.00
(a)	4.50

Cash out	£m
Expenditure on office building and equipment	0.10
Purchases of T-shirts from suppliers paid for in cash	2.00
Salaries	0.20
Rent and business rates	0.20
Advertising fees	0.28
(b)	2.78

The cash balance at the end of July 1998 is (a) minus (b) which equals £1.72 million.

We are now in a position to summarize Michael Owen Limited's total assets. The situation is as follows:

Assets	£m
Office building and equipment	0.10
Trade debtors	1.00
Pre-payment (business rates)	0.02
Cash balance	1.72
Total assets	**2.84**

Notes

The office building and equipment are called 'fixed assets' as they are expected to be kept in the business *for more than a year.*

The other assets, the trade debtors, the pre-payment and the cash balance, are referred to as 'current assets'. They are assets which are either in the form of cash or which can be converted easily into cash within 12 months of the balance sheet date.

Total assets are equal to fixed assets of £0.1 million plus current assets of £2.74 million, giving £2.84 million.

Most assets are stated in the balance sheet at what is called their *historic cost*. Historic cost is simply the cost of the asset at the time when it was acquired.

Liabilities (what the company owes)
1. Amount due to the suppliers of T-shirts, called trade creditors: £800,000.
2. Unpaid advertising bill: £70,000.
3. Other liabilities: there are no additional *external* liabilities or creditors. However, we need to consider two new aspects. First, Michael Owen contributed £500,000 when the business started. Second, during its first year of trading, the business earned an operating profit of £1.47 million. Both these amounts are attributable to the shareholder. They are part of the financing of the business and are referred to as the shareholder's equity.

A summary of the total liabilities at the end of July 1998 is as follows:

Liabilities	£m
Amounts due to the suppliers of T-shirts	0.80
Unpaid advertising bill (an accrued charge)	0.07
	0.87
Shareholder's equity	
Opening share capital	0.50
Profit for the year ended 31 July 1998	1.47
	1.97
Total liabilities	**2.84**

Notes

Amounts due to suppliers and the unpaid advertising bill are examples of current liabilities. These are liabilities or commitments which have to be paid off within 12 months of the balance sheet date.

The shareholder's equity (£1.97 million) is the most permanent part of the financing of a business. It is sometimes referred to as the *risk capital* since it cannot be paid back to shareholders – the owners of the business – until all other external commitments such as bank loans and amounts due to suppliers have been discharged. It may seem strange that the shareholder's equity is treated as a liability. However, don't forget that the balance sheet is being prepared from the point of view of Michael Owen Limited which is a separate legal entity, quite distinct from the shareholder. The shareholder's equity belongs to the shareholder. From the company's point of view, it is a financial obligation.

You will notice that the effect of earning a profit is to increase the shareholder's equity. When Michael Owen started his business, the equity was just £500,000, the opening capital contribution. At the end of the first 12 months, the shareholder's equity had risen to £1.97 million. The difference of £1.47 million is the profit earned during the year to the end of July 1998.

Presentation
The balance sheet of Michael Owen Limited can now be presented in a vertical format as shown below. The figures are exactly the same. It is simply a matter of a revised presentation.

Michael Owen Limited
Balance Sheet as at 31 July 1998 (£m)

Fixed assets	
Office building and equipment	0.10
Current assets	
Trade debtors	1.00
Pre-payment	0.02
Cash balance	1.72
	2.74
Current liabilities	
Trade creditors	0.80
Accrued charge	0.07
	0.87
Net current assets	1.87
Total assets less current liabilities	**1.97**
Financed by:	
Shareholder's equity:	
Share capital	0.50
Profit for the year ended 31 July 1998	1.47
	1.97

Notes
The difference between current assets (£2.74 million) and current liabilities (£0.87 million) is £1.87 million. This is referred to as *net current assets* or *working capital*. It represents the short-term assets invested in the business to enable it to trade. The short-term assets are changing from day to day according to the nature and the volume of the business undertaken.

Total assets less current liabilities is referred to as *capital employed*. You will also notice that total assets less current liabilities is equivalent to fixed assets plus current assets less current liabilities. This is the same as fixed assets plus working capital.

SUMMARY

The profit and loss account/income statement

It is concerned with financial performance over a given period of time to answer the question 'How much profit has the business earned?'

- Profit equals the revenues or sales or turnover generated less the costs incurred.
- Earning a profit and generating cash are not the same thing. As we have seen, revenues are recognized when goods or services are provided to customers, not when the cash is received from them. Costs are recognized when they are incurred, not when the cash is paid out.

The balance sheet

A description of what a business *owns* (called assets) and what it *owes* (called liabilities) at a particular date.

- The focus is on financial position. What are the company's assets? How have these assets been financed?
- Don't forget that, because of the dual aspect convention, assets must always equal liabilities. Every accounting transaction has two equal and opposite elements.

CHAPTER 4

An Introduction to the Cash Flow Statement

DEFINITION

We have seen that the profit and loss account is concerned with revenues and costs and the balance sheet highlights assets and liabilities. However, the financial picture is not quite complete since we have not yet drawn attention to cash flows or the cash effects of the various transactions carried out by the business. We need to be able to answer such questions as, how has the business financed its capital expenditure (expenditure on fixed assets) and to what extent has it had to rely on bank borrowings and further contributions from shareholders? A cash flow statement focuses on these matters by presenting information from both the balance sheet and the profit and loss account in a different way. The objective is to explain how cash, bank balances and borrowings have changed during a particular period and to understand the reasons why.

EXAMPLE

Michael Owen Limited for the year to 31 July 1998.

Sources of cash

(a) Opening capital contribution from Michael Owen: £500,000.
(b) Operating profit: £1.47 million. Being profitable helps cash flow, but it is not the same as cash flow. There are timing differences between the recognition of revenues and the receipt of cash, and the recog

nition of costs and the payment of cash. This is allowed for by including changes in working capital – the trade debtors, the pre-payment, trade creditors, and the accrued charge figures.

(c) Unpaid bills: £800,000 is owed to suppliers and £70,000 is owed for an unpaid advertising bill. This totals £870,000 and represents an indirect source of cash since the business is taking credit and post-poning the payment.

Therefore, the total sources of cash are (a) plus (b) plus (c) which equals £2.84 million.

Uses of cash

(d) Expenditure on the office building and equipment: £100,000.
(e) Cash not yet received and the pre-payment: £1 million is owed by customers and £20,000 has been paid in advance for business rates. This totals £1.02 million and represents an indirect payment of cash since the business is allowing credit and making an advance payment.

Therefore, the total usage is (d) plus (e) which equals £1.12 million.

Cash summary

	£m
Sources	2.84
Uses	(1.12)
Cash balance in Michael Owen's balance sheet as at 31 July 1998	1.72

THE RELATIONSHIPS BETWEEN PROFIT AND LOSS ACCOUNTS, BALANCE SHEETS AND CASH FLOW STATEMENTS

These are summarized in Figure 4.1. Michael Owen Limited started to trade on 1 August 1997 using the £500,000 share capital it received from Michael Owen. This allowed the business to incur costs and to generate revenues as summarized in the profit and loss account for the year to the end of July 1998. As a result of both financing and trading transactions, the company also generated cash inflows and outflows as summarized in the cash flow statement. Finally, at the end of the financial year, a closing balance sheet was prepared to describe the company's assets and liabilities after its first year of selling T-shirts.

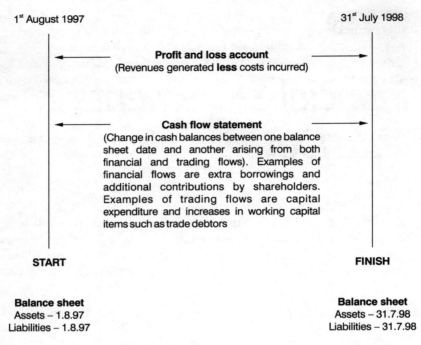

Figure 4.1   *The relationships between profit and loss accounts, balance sheets and cash flow statements*

SUMMARY

Three financial statements are needed to fully describe a company's business activities: the profit and loss account, the cash flow statement and the balance sheet.

The profit and loss account answers the question 'Is the business profitable?' The cash flow statement answers the question 'To what extent has the business generated cash?' The balance sheet answers the question 'Is the business soundly financed?'

Earning a profit and generating cash are not synonymous in view of the timing differences between recognizing revenues and receiving cash, and incurring costs and paying cash. Also, for perfectly valid reasons, the calculation of profit is not entirely straightforward since estimates, especially of costs, will need to be made. Profit is, therefore, a matter of opinion, whereas cash is a matter of fact. You either have it or you don't!

PART II

Financial Statements in More Detail

CHAPTER 5

The Profit and Loss Account in More Detail

INTRODUCTION

In Chapter 2, we spent some time explaining the meaning of a profit and loss account and its basic structure. The purpose of this chapter is to look at the profit and loss account in more detail. First, we will look at a number of specific points such as depreciation, the cost of sales and taxation. Second, we will look at Unilever's 1997 profit and loss account to explain a real example.

DEPRECIATION

You may recall that Michael Owen Limited spent £20,000 on office equipment for the year to the end of July 1998. Let us suppose that the estimated useful life of the equipment is four years. It would be quite unfair to treat the whole of this £20,000 as a cost in the 1997/98 profit and loss account since the benefits of using the office equipment are estimated to last four years. Instead, the charge should be spread over this extended period using the process of depreciation. There are several ways in which this can be done. The most common and the most straightforward is to charge an equal instalment for each year of the equipment's life. This is called the 'straight-line' method. The depreciation charged works out at £5,000 a year (the £20,000 cost divided by four years). Don't forget that the depreciation process applies only to fixed assets – those assets that are expected to be in use for at least one year from the balance sheet date.

There are a number of important points to remember about depreciation. First, no cash is involved. Michael Owen paid £20,000 to acquire the equipment during the 1997/98 financial year. That was when the cash was spent. Second, even though the £5,000 annual depreciation charge does not involve any cash outflow, it is as much a part of Michael Owen's operating costs as advertising and salaries.

In the case of Michael Owen, the revised profit and loss account including depreciation for the year ended 31 July 1998 will be as follows:

	£000s
Revenues	5,000
Cost of products sold	(2,800)
Gross profit	**2,200**
Operating costs	
Advertising	(350)
Salaries	(200)
Rent and rates	(180)
Depreciation	(5)
	(735)
Operating profit	**1,465**

Impact on the balance sheet

The amount shown in the balance sheet will be the cost of the office equipment less the amount of the accumulated depreciation at the end of the relevant financial year. For example, at 31 July 1998:

	£000s
Office equipment at cost	20
Less accumulated depreciation	(5)
Net book value or written down value	15

As the life of the office equipment goes beyond its first year, depreciation will be reported as follows:

Year	Accumulated depreciation at start of year (£)	Profit and loss account for the year (£)	Accumulated depreciation at end of year (£)	Net book value at end of year (£)
2 (1999)	5,000	5,000	10,000	10,000
3 (2000)	10,000	5,000	15,000	5,000
4 (2001)	15,000	5,000	20,000	–

It is most unlikely that the net book value (NBV) at the end of the fourth year is what Michael Owen will expect to obtain for the office equipment when it is sold. Zero is the accounting 'value' based on the result of the depreciation process. It is not the same as the office equipment's market or realizable value. If it is sold for, say, £1,000 there will be a profit on disposal of £1,000 (£1,000 less the book value of zero). This profit can either be deducted from the depreciation charge of the other assets or shown separately in the profit and loss account.

An alternative way of working out the depreciation for the office equipment is to estimate what is called the 'residual value' at the end of its useful life. For example, this may be £2,000. The depreciation process is, therefore, based on the difference between the original cost of £20,000 and the estimated residual value of £2,000 at the end of year four (31 July 2001). The depreciation charge each year will be £20,000 less £2,000 divided by four to give £4,500. In the balance sheet at the end of year two, for example (31 July 1999), the net book value of the equipment will be £20,000 less two years of depreciation, £9,000, which is £11,000. At the end of the fourth year, the NBV will be £2,000 which is exactly the same as the estimated residual value. Whether it is in practice, is quite another matter!

Different kinds of fixed assets will have different commercial lives. In the case of Unilever, for example, plant and equipment are depreciated or written off over a period of between four and 20 years, motor vehicles are written off over a period of between three and six years. The straight-line method is used in both cases.

Apart from the straight-line method, there are a number of others such as the reducing balance method and the sum of the digits method. However, they are much less common.

REVENUE EXPENDITURE AND CAPITAL EXPENDITURE

All expenditure is described as either revenue or capital expenditure. Revenue expenditure refers to expenditure incurred on day-to-day activities such as administration, advertising, raw materials and salaries. It is charged straight away in the profit and loss account according to the time period to which it relates.

By contrast, capital expenditure refers to expenditure on longer-term (more than one year) purposes such as investments in plant and machinery and joint ventures. Such expenditure is 'capitalized' in the balance sheet and depreciated over its estimated commercial life according to the process of depreciation.

There are some 'grey' areas which make the distinction between revenue expenditure and capital expenditure difficult to determine. One of the classic examples is maintenance. If maintenance is defined as revenue expenditure, there is an immediate 'hit' to the profit and loss account. If, however, it is defined as capital expenditure the impact will be spread over several financial periods. Although the distinction is important for the purposes of calculating profit, it is not relevant from the point of view of cash. That has to be spent regardless of whether the costs involved are revenue or capital items!

COST OF SALES AND STOCK

When goods are manufactured or purchased for resale, they are rarely all sold in the same financial period. This gives rise, therefore, to stocks at the end of one financial period and the start of another. As we have seen, a basic principle of the profit and loss account is that revenues or sales must be matched with the cost of those same sales.

The adjustments for changing stock levels are shown in the trading section of the profit and loss account. Here is an example:

Atherton Ltd – Trading account for the year ended 31 October 1998

	£
Sales	100,000
Cost of sales	
Opening stock	40,000
Purchases	50,000
	90,000
Less closing stock	(35,000)
	55,000
Gross profit	**£45,000**

Manufacturing companies such as British Aerospace and General Electric of North America will not just have stocks of finished goods but also raw materials and partly finished goods which are called 'work in progress'. Opening and closing stocks for these items are adjusted in a similar way to that shown for Atherton Ltd when manufacturing costs are calculated for a financial period.

FORMAT OF A PROFIT AND LOSS ACCOUNT

Michael Owen Limited's profit and loss account for the year ended 31 July 1998 is shown below.

	£000s
Revenues	5,000
Cost of sales	(2,800)
Gross profit	**2,200**
Operating costs	
Advertising	(350)
Salaries	(200)
Rent and rates	(180)
Depreciation	(5)
	(735)
Operating profit	**1,465**

But this is not the complete version since two items are missing: interest charges and taxation. Just for the purposes of illustration, assume that interest charges are £465,000 and that taxation is £500,000. The complete version of the profit and loss account for Michael Owen is now as follows:

	£000s
Revenues	5,000
Cost of sales	(2,800)
Gross profit	**2,200**
Operating costs	
Advertising	(350)
Salaries	(200)
Rent and rates	(180)
Depreciation	(5)
	(735)
Operating profit	**1,465**
Interest charges	(465)
Profit before taxation	**1,000**
Taxation	(500)
Profit after taxation	**500**

Notes

The operating profit less the interest charges is referred to as the profit before taxation (PBT).

Profit before taxation less taxation is equal, of course, to the profit after taxation.

Another expression for profit after taxation (PAT) is 'earnings' or, in the USA, 'net income'. This is the 'bottom line' since it is the profit earned by the business after deducting all costs.

TAXATION

Corporation tax is the system which applies to the profits of all limited companies.

The Inland Revenue does not recognize the depreciation charge disclosed by a company in its profit and loss account regardless of which depreciation method is used. This is because the Revenue has its own system of tax allowances which acts as a substitute for depreciation.

There is one standard rate of corporation tax. Currently, it is 31 per cent but it will be reduced to 30 per cent with effect from April 1999. Small and medium-sized companies, defined as those with taxable profits of less than £1.5 million per year, pay corporation tax at a reduced rate. The current minimum rate is 21 per cent which will be lowered to 20 per cent from April 1999. The profit on which corporation tax is levied is not the same as the profit before taxation disclosed in the profit and loss account. Instead, it is an adjusted figure after some costs have been disallowed and capital allowances used in place of the depreciation charge. For this reason, companies cannot manipulate their tax charge by changing depreciation policy. The Inland Revenue will add back whatever depreciation a company charges. For example:

Seaman Ltd – Year ended 31 December 1998

	£m
Profit before tax as shown in the profit and loss account	10.0
Add back disallowable items:	
Depreciation	2.0
Entertainment	0.2
Political contributions	0.1
	2.3
	12.3
Deduct capital allowances	(3.3)
Taxable profit	**9.0**

The corporation tax payable is £9.0 million × 31 per cent = £2.79 million.

Capital allowances are based on two systems which are applied to different assets, and the size of the allowances varies from time to time. The current ones are:

Industrial buildings (such as a factory): 4 per cent per annum on a straight line basis for 25 years.

Plant and equipment: 25 per cent on a reducing balance basis ('long life' assets with an expected working life of 25 years or more are given capital allowances at 6 per cent per year). This means, for example, that in 'year 2', on plant costing £10 million, the capital allowance will be 25 per cent times £10 million less £2.5 million, which is £1.875 million.

One of the consequences of the differences between tax allowances and depreciation is that companies pay less tax than the standard rate of corporation tax on their pre-tax profits. This is the case with Seaman Ltd (27.9 per cent rather than 31 per cent), because the capital allowances exceed the depreciation charge. However, that may not continue indefinitely especially if the level of capital expenditure is expected to fall. If such a situation is expected to occur, an extra allowance or provision is made by charging the additional tax in the profit and loss account now. This additional tax is called 'deferred taxation'. It is disclosed as a long-term liability in the balance sheet since it is expected to be paid at least 12 months after the balance sheet date.

PROVISIONS

We have just referred to a provision for deferred taxation. A provision is similar to an accrued charge. The difference is that whereas an accrued charge such as an unpaid telephone bill is known very accurately, a provision is not. It refers to a future liability which is expected to occur, but the amount and, possibly, the date of payment are uncertain. Quite apart from deferred taxation, there are other kinds of long-term provisions. For example, in the year to the end of March 1998, Marks & Spencer disclosed a provision of nearly £28m for post-retirement health benefits. It has a commitment to pay health insurance premiums to some of its retired employees. A number of companies such as Reckitt and Colman have also made large provisions for 'Year 2000' costs.

It is important to appreciate that including a provision in the profit and loss account and as a liability in the balance sheet has no immediate effect on cash. Cash payments will be made at some time in the future. Often, there is loose terminology in connection with provisions. *The Financial Times*, for example, sometimes reports that 'money has been laid aside to meet future commitments'. That is not the case! An additional charge has been included in the profit and loss account and an equivalent liability set up in the balance sheet.

Another reason for mentioning the importance of provisions is connected with the accounting convention of 'prudence'. This stipulates that profits should not be anticipated, for example, by including in sales unsold stock at the end of a financial period. It also means that provisions should be made without delay for all known liabilities and anticipated losses. This principle applies even if the amounts involved and the timing can only be estimated. The message is: anticipate the bad news and wait for the good news so that unpleasant surprises can be avoided!

EXAMPLE

The information below is taken from Unilever's Annual Report for the 1997 calendar year.

Unilever Group
Consolidated profit and loss account for the year ended 31 December 1997 (£m)

Turnover	29,766
Cost of sales	(16,477)
Gross profit	**13,289**
Operating costs	(10,338)
Operating profit	**2,951**
Exceptional items:	
Reorganization costs	(565)
Profit on the sale of a major business	2,383
	1,818
Operating profit after exceptional items	**4,769**
Net interest charges	(46)
Profit on ordinary activities before taxation	**4,723**
Taxation	(1,291)
Profit on ordinary activities after taxation	**3,432**
Minority interests	(97)
Net profit after taxation	**3,335**
Preference dividends	(5)
Earnings – the profit attributable to ordinary shareholders	3,330
Ordinary dividends	(719)

Retained profit for the year	2,611
Earnings per share	45p

The word 'consolidated' or 'group' as part of the title of the profit and loss account indicates that the Unilever group owns at least 50 per cent of the voting share capital of a number of companies. These companies are called 'subsidiaries'. For example, it owns 80 per cent of Lyons Tea in Ireland. In the preparation of a consolidated profit and loss account, the revenues and costs of all the subsidiaries are included. This is because the group fully controls the subsidiaries from a management point of view, even if it does not fully own them.

Turnover

This is the invoiced value of all the goods and services provided by Unilever to its external customers. It is calculated after deducting any sales discounts and value added tax (VAT). In the case of VAT, Unilever acts as a collection agent on behalf of the government. Therefore, there will be an amount owed to the government, which will be a short-term creditor or an amount due from the government, which will be a short-term debtor.

Cost of sales

This is the direct cost of the sales made by Unilever to its customers. It includes raw materials and packaging (which account for nearly 80 per cent of the total cost of sales). More generally, it will also include the cost of the labour involved in manufacturing the products.

Gross profit

This is the difference between revenue, turnover or sales, and the cost of sales. It is an indicator of the basic profitability of the goods and services sold. The gross profit needs to be large enough to cover at least operating costs, interest charges and taxation so as to provide an adequate level of earnings.

Operating costs

These are the costs involved in running the business. In the case of Unilever and other companies, they include distribution and selling costs, staff costs, depreciation, advertising and promotion, research and development, legal fees and the remuneration of the auditors.

The difference between the gross profit and operating costs is the operating profit or the profit before interest and taxation. It is the profit earned directly by the business from its trading activities.

Exceptional items

These are unusual items, which need to be distinguished from normal items such as ongoing operating costs. They are shown separately so that the underlying performance can be assessed as well as the overall result. It may be possible, for example, to show an excellent underlying result but the result overall was affected by abnormal costs or gains such as:

- major reorganization (as in the case of Unilever);
- the profit on the sale of a business (Unilever again);
- significant redundancy costs;
- a loss on the sale of a business.

The requirement to disclose exceptional items separately was made in Financial Reporting Standard 3 (FRS3) 'Reporting Financial Performance', published in October 1992.

Net interest charge

This is the difference between the interest payable on borrowings and the interest receivable. Interest receivable materializes, for example, by placing surplus cash balances on the short-term money markets to earn a return.

Profit on ordinary activities before taxation

The key term here is 'ordinary activities'. FRS3 has defined them as almost every conceivable activity or event that occurs during a company's life! This is irrespective of their frequency or unusual nature. FRS3 also requires companies to identify revenues and costs for continuing operations, acquisitions and discontinued operations.

Taxation

This is the tax charge for the year following a separate calculation of taxable profits. It includes a provision for the tax arising on the profit earned outside the UK.

Minority interest

Many subsidiary companies such as the Unilever Group's 80 per cent interest in Lyons Tea Ireland are not fully owned. This means that there are shareholders in Lyons Tea who are not shareholders in Unilever. More generally, subsidiary companies are partly owned by minority shareholders. They are the shareholders who hold shares in the subsidiary only. They are referred to as the 'minority interest'.

In the case of Unilever, the minority interest's figure of £97 million represents the share of the profit after taxation owned by the minorities and not the Unilever Group. Therefore, it needs to be deducted to arrive at the Group's net profit after taxation of £3,335 million.

Preference dividends

These are the dividends paid to preference shareholders who, unlike ordinary shareholders, are not the owners of the business. Preference dividends must be paid before ordinary dividends, hence the word 'preferred'. Generally, they are a fixed amount for each preference share.

Earnings (the profit attributable to the ordinary shareholders)

As mentioned earlier, this is the 'bottom line'. It is the profit after taxation and all other charges less the minority interest and preference dividends.

Ordinary dividends

This is the amount recommended by the directors, subject to approval by shareholders, to be distributed to ordinary shareholders. The ordinary shareholders are the owners of the business. The ordinary dividend varies with the fortunes of the business. It is dependent both on the level of earnings and the amount of cash available. Most dividends are paid out in cash. They are an appropriation of and not a charge against earnings. A dividend is an appropriation in the profit and loss account and, if it is unpaid, a current liability described as a 'proposed dividend' in the balance sheet. When the dividend is paid in cash, the company's cash balance will be reduced and the proposed dividend will be removed from the balance sheet.

Retained profit for the year

This is the difference between the earnings and the ordinary dividends. It increases the equity or shareholders' section of the balance sheet by the amount involved.

The statement of total recognized gains and losses

The purpose of this statement is to include, in one report, details of all the gains and losses of the period and thus show total financial performance. Some transactions such as the revaluation of a property will not appear in the profit and loss account because they are of a non-trading nature. The same is true of changes in the sterling value of overseas assets and liabilities due to exchange rate fluctuations.

In the case of Unilever, for the year to the end of 1997, the statement is made up of the net profit before preference dividends of £3,335 million less the adverse effects of exchange rate fluctuations of £339 million. This resulted in total recognized gains of £2,996 million.

Earnings per share (EPS)

EPS is calculated by dividing the profit attributable to the ordinary shareholders by the number of issued ordinary shares. In the case of Unilever, the earnings for the 1997 calendar year were £3,330 million. There are nearly 7.5 billion issued ordinary shares so that the EPS works out at nearly 45p.

The FRS3 definition of EPS includes all realized gains and losses. But this means that the comparison of performance between companies may be difficult. This occurs when there are exceptional items of a capital nature such as the profit or loss on the sale of a business. In the case of Unilever, for example, there was an exceptional capital profit of nearly £2.4 billion from the disposal of its speciality chemicals business. This accounted for 32p of its total EPS of 45p and distorted the EPS arising from underlying trading performance.

For this reason, the Institute of Investment Management and Research (IIMR) has produced a 'headline' earnings definition which excludes any capital items. *The Financial Times* uses the IIMR definition.

SUMMARY

There are a number of detailed aspects to a profit and loss account.

Depreciation is the process of spreading the cost of a fixed or capital asset over its expected useful life. The most common method is the straight-line method. Depreciation has no direct effect on cash. Cash is paid out when the asset is acquired and received when the asset is sold. Depreciation is not allowable for tax purposes.

Revenue expenditure is expenditure on day-to-day items such as salaries and wages. By contrast, *capital expenditure* is for the longer term – at least a year – and refers to expenditure on plant, machinery and buildings.

The *cost of sales* is the direct cost of the products and services sold and includes items such as labour, materials and packaging.

To complete a profit and loss account, all expenses including *interest charges* and *taxation* should be considered. The 'bottom line' is the profit after taxation, or earnings ('net income' in North America). *Corporation tax* is the tax levied on companies. It is worked out separately because some items are allowable for tax purposes and others, notably depreciation, are not.

The term *provision* needs careful explanation. It is an estimated allowance for a future liability such as 'Year 2000' costs, which is charged to the profit and loss account and set up as an obligation in the balance sheet.

A published profit and loss account such as Unilever's follows a standard format. The word *consolidated* means that the financial statements of the subsidiary companies in the Group have been added together and an adjustment, called the 'minority interest', has been made for those businesses which are not fully owned.

Earnings per share (EPS) is an important statistic. It is calculated by dividing the earnings by the number of issued ordinary shares.

CHAPTER 6

The Balance Sheet in More Detail

INTRODUCTION

The purpose of this chapter is to consider the balance sheet of a leading international business. The consolidated balance sheet of the Unilever Group as at 31 December 1997 is shown below.

EXAMPLE

Unilever plc as at 31 December 1997

	£m
Fixed assets	
Tangible fixed assets	6,009
Fixed investments	98
	6,107
Current assets	
Stocks	3,111
Debtors due within one year	3,453
Debtors due after more than one year	723
Current investments	2,511
Cash balances	3,342
	13,140
Creditors due within one year	
Borrowings	941
Trade and other creditors	5,555
	6,496

Net current assets	6,644
Total assets less current liabilities	**12,751**
Financed by	
Share capital and reserves	7,416
Minority interests	312
Creditors due after more than one year	
Borrowings	1,729
Trade and other creditors	447
	2,176
Provisions for liabilities and charges	
Pensions and similar obligations	1,934
Other provisions	913
	2,847
Total capital employed	**12,751**

The word 'consolidated' or 'group' as part of the title of the balance sheet indicates that the Unilever Group owns at least 50 per cent of the voting share capital of a number of companies. These companies are called 'subsidiaries'. In the preparation of a consolidated balance sheet, all the assets and liabilities of the subsidiaries are included.

The capital provided by the minority shareholders in the subsidiaries is recognized separately as part of the financing of the group. It is called 'minority interest'.

HISTORICAL COST ACCOUNTING (HCA)

The Unilever Group's balance sheet is prepared under the historical cost convention. This simply means that assets are disclosed at their original cost less the accumulated depreciation. The use of HCA does not preclude the revaluation of certain assets, notably land and buildings. But it does mean that some balance sheets are a bit of an accounting 'fruit salad'! Some assets are based on HCA and others on their open market value as in the case of properties. Marks & Spencer is an example of a company following this kind of practice.

HCA has the effect of understating asset values owing to the impact of inflation. Also, it overstates profit in the profit and loss account since the depreciation charge, which is based on the original cost of the asset, is too low. In the case of Unilever, for the year to the end of December 1997, its fixed assets would have been 17 per cent higher on what is called a 'current cost' basis. The change in the depreciation charge would have been even more significant. It would have been 27 per cent higher.

It is important to realize that a balance sheet is not a statement of value. It does not indicate what a business is worth. A balance sheet is simply a statement summarizing a company's assets and liabilities at a particular date. These assets and liabilities are stated at amounts based on accounting conventions, especially historic cost.

The assumption is that the group or company as a whole is not for sale, although certain parts of it may be disposed of during the course of the financial year. (Unilever, for example, sold its speciality chemicals business to ICI during 1997.) This assumption refers to the 'going concern' principle. In the case of Unilever and other companies, the directors highlight in their Statement of Directors' Responsibilities that the 'going concern' basis has been adopted in preparing the financial statements. It means that the directors consider that the group has adequate cash resources and borrowing facilities to meet its commitments for the foreseeable future.

FIXED ASSETS

Tangible fixed assets

These are the physical long-term assets that are expected to be used in the business for at least a year. In the case of Unilever, they include freehold and leasehold land (£1,913 million) and plant and machinery (£4,096 million). These amounts are stated at historic cost less the accumulated depreciation. The details of the location, historic cost and accumulated depreciation of each fixed asset are maintained in what is called a 'fixed asset register'.

The practice of depreciating fixed assets also applies to some leased assets. There are two sorts of leases. An operating lease applies to the hire of plant and machinery for a short period such as a few weeks or a couple of months. At the end of the period, the equipment is returned to the hire company. Operating lease or hire charges are charged to the profit and loss account as and when they are incurred. The assets concerned do not appear on the balance sheet. A finance lease is similar to hire purchase. However, there may be no purchase option at the end of the lease term. It is a long-term contract to hire fixed assets. The full capital value of the leased asset is shown or capitalized on the balance sheet with the commitment to the lessor split between short- and long-term creditors. The asset is depreciated each year by the amount of the annual capital repayments. Interest charges on the lease agreement are included in the profit and loss account as they are incurred.

Fixed investments

These refer to Unilever's investment in companies that are not subsidiaries. For example, there are associated companies. Unilever does not control the business concerned since its ownership of the voting share capital lies somewhere between 20 and 50 per cent. The results of these companies are not consolidated or included in the group accounts. Instead, Unilever records its share of the associates' after-tax profits in the group profit and loss account (for the sake of simplicity, we have not shown them separately because the amounts involved are relatively small).

In cases where the ownership of the share capital lies between 0 and 20 per cent, the investment is called a 'trade investment'. The group owning the trade investment – not relevant in the case of Unilever – only records its share of the dividends received in the group profit and loss account.

CURRENT ASSETS

Stocks

Stocks are valued at their historical cost or realizable value, whichever is the lower. For example, if the market value of a commodity such as cocoa or oil is lower than the original purchase cost, this will result in a stock loss and a fall in operating profit. The valuation of work in progress and finished goods at cost is more complicated. The direct cost of labour and materials is part of the cost. So too is a proportion of the indirect costs such as lighting and electricity. The issue is, what proportion? Guidelines are available in *Standard Statement of Accounting Practice*, no 9 on 'Stocks and work in progress'. It was originally published in May 1975, with major revisions in September 1988.

In the case of Unilever, finished goods represented 56 per cent of the total stock value of £3,111 million.

Debtors due within one year

These refer to amounts due from third parties. The most important category is trade debtors, or 'amounts receivable' to use the US term. Trade debtors are customers who have been invoiced for credit sales and who have not yet paid. The basis for valuing trade debtors is to take the full amount of all the sales invoices outstanding. A provision, called a bad debt provision, is then deducted from this value to allow for possible bad debts. The provision is based on past experience and the

age of the amount outstanding. Most companies have internal proce-
dures so that if an amount outstanding is between, say, three and four
months old, a bad debt provision of, say, 2 per cent may be applied. The
bad debt provision is charged as an expense in the profit and loss
account. It is also deducted from the full value of the trade debtor so that
the amount stated in the balance sheet for trade debtors is after
deducting the bad debt provision. In Unilever's case, this comes to
£2,545 million.

The other debtors due within a year are pre-payments – payments
made in advance of goods and services being received – such as utility
bills for electricity and telephones. This comes to £908 million, so that
the total debtors' figure in the balance sheet is £3,453 million (£2,545
million plus £908 million).

Debtors due after more than one year

These are also amounts due from third parties. However, they are not
expected to be received until January 1999 at the earliest. Strictly
speaking, therefore, they are not current assets since the cash will not be
forthcoming within 12 months of the balance sheet date. For Unilever,
the amounts involved are pre-payments made into pension schemes and
corporation tax recoverable from the government. The total is £723
million.

Current investments

These are short-term investments such as money market deposits and
government securities. They indicate that a business has surplus cash on
which it needs to earn an acceptable rate of return before it is used for
longer-term purposes such as capital expenditure and business acquisitions. For Unilever, the amount involved exceeds £2.5 billion.

Cash balances

These consist of cash balances in hand or immediately available (£663
million) and cash balances at banks for which notice of repayment is
required (£2,679 million), totalling £3,342 million. They are similar to
current investments although the notice period for repayment is likely to
be shorter.

The combination of current investments and cash balances is sometimes referred to as 'liquid resources'. BP, for example, uses this term. It
is the corporate treasury function's responsibility to ensure that liquid
resources are managed effectively.

CREDITORS DUE WITHIN ONE YEAR (OR CURRENT LIABILITIES)

These refer to amounts due for payment by Unilever within 12 months of the balance sheet date.

Borrowings

A typical form of short-term borrowing is a bank overdraft, which is repayable on demand or without notice. Other types are short-term bank loans and a bond. A bond is a written promise to pay the bondholder a specified sum at an agreed date and at a stated rate of interest. For Unilever, short-term loans and overdrafts amounted to £546 million and bonds £395 million, to give total short-term borrowings of £941 million.

Trade and other creditors

'Trade creditors' refers to amounts due to suppliers for the goods they have provided, such as raw materials. Other creditors include such items as accrued charges, corporation tax, PAYE, national insurance contributions, proposed dividends and VAT. All these items came to £5,555 million.

NET CURRENT ASSETS (OR WORKING CAPITAL)

This is the difference between current assets and current liabilities. In the case of Unilever, it is £6,644 million. It represents the net investment in short-term assets to finance day-to-day operations. The French term is *fonds de roulement* or 'rolling funds', to indicate that they circulate through the business every day.

A positive figure for working capital means that short-term creditors finance a proportion of the current assets. It is only the net current assets that need to be financed from long-term sources such as bank borrowings and share capital.

CAPITAL EMPLOYED

Total assets less current liabilities

This is equal to the sum of fixed assets and current assets less current liabilities. Another expression with the same meaning is 'capital employed'. For Unilever, the figure as at the end of December 1997 was £12,751 million.

FINANCING

We now turn our attention to the financing of Unilever. This will enable us to identify the sources from which its assets were acquired. In the case of limited companies, there are two main sources: shareholders and borrowings.

Share capital and reserves

Ordinary share capital represents the risk or equity capital of every company. It is the permanent capital contributed directly by the owners both at the start of trading and later, when additional capital is needed to finance expansion. The issued or called-up share capital is the amount of capital contributed by shareholders and received by the company. It is the value of shares issued at their nominal or par value. Shares which are issued at a price in excess of this nominal value create what is called a 'share premium reserve'. This is what happens at a 'rights' issue when new shares are sold to current shareholders in proportion to their existing holdings. New shares tend to be issued at a discount to their current value to encourage shareholders to take up their 'rights'. A very different type of share issue is called a 'scrip' issue or a bonus issue. This is a free issue of new shares to existing shareholders in proportion to their current holdings. No new share capital is received and no cash is raised. A company simply converts some or all of its retained profit into share capital. Since the number of ordinary shares has increased, the share price will fall pro rata. Companies arrange scrip issues to increase the marketability of their shares.

Authorized capital is the total amount of share capital which the directors are empowered to issue. For Unilever, it is £437 million.

Ordinary shares have no fixed dividend rate so that dividend distributions usually follow the trend in earnings. Only a proportion of the earnings is normally paid out in the form of dividends. The balance is the profit retained for the year and it is added to the shareholders' interest. In the case of Unilever, the issued ordinary share capital is £94 million. The nominal value of each share is 1.25p. The share premium reserve is £110 million.

Preference shares have priority over ordinary shares both for dividends and any capital repayments. Preference dividends are paid at a fixed percentage of the nominal value of the preferred shares. For

Unilever, the percentages are 5, 6 and 7 per cent. For cumulative preference shares, all past unpaid dividends must be paid before an ordinary share dividend is paid. Unilever has issued cumulative preference shares, with a nominal value of £80 million.

Reserves

This is the most misleading term in accounting! It has nothing whatever to do with cash. Instead, reserves represent realized and unrealized gains that have added value to the business. They form part of the shareholders' equity or the shareholders' interest. Realized gains produce profits, which after dividends give retained profit. Unrealized gains arise from the revaluation of assets such as property. And, as we have seen, a third form of gain is the share premium, which is the excess of the value of issued new shares over their nominal value.

Unilever's overall share capital and reserves may, therefore, be summarized as follows:

	£m
Issued share capital	
Ordinary	94
Preference	80
	174
Share premium account	110
	284
Retained profit	7,132
	7,416

The £7,416 million is sometimes referred to as the 'book value' or the net asset value of the business.

Minority interests

The meaning of minority interests was referred to earlier. The amount attributable to these minority shareholders in Unilever's subsidiaries was £312 million. It is less than 3 per cent of the group's total capital employed.

Creditors due after more than one year

These consist of borrowings that are not due for repayment until at least a year after the balance sheet date (£1,729 million), and commitments such as corporation tax which do not fall due for payment until 1999 at the earliest (£447 million).

Provisions for liabilities and charges

As we have mentioned, provisions are made without delay for estimated losses and/or costs that are expected to occur at some time in the future. These provisions are charged as an expense in the profit and loss account and a liability for the same amount is set up in the balance sheet. In due course, these provisions are 'utilized'. This means that cash payments are made against them so that the provisions will fall unless additional ones are created to take account of new liabilities.

If the provisions turn out to be inadequate, the extra amount required will be charged as a cost in the profit and loss account during the financial period when the shortfall becomes apparent. If the provisions should exceed the actual cost incurred then the excess will be 'released' by reducing costs and increasing profit during the financial period when the excess becomes evident.

As you can see from Unilever's balance sheet, there are two major provisions. One is for future pensions obligations (£1,934 million). The other is for 'restructuring provisions' to cover the expected future costs of reorganizing the business (£913 million).

SUMMARY

A consolidated balance sheet is the sum of all the assets and liabilities of a group of subsidiary companies owned by the parent company. An adjustment is then made to show the 'minority interest' separately.

The value of assets in a balance sheet is usually based on historical cost less accumulated depreciation. However, some assets such as property may be valued at their 'open market value'.

A balance sheet is not a statement of value. It does not tell you how much a business is worth since the 'value' of the assets disclosed is based on accounting conventions, principally historical cost, rather than the prices at which they could be disposed of.

Unilever's balance sheet follows a standardized format and, as we shall see in greater detail later (Chapter 8), particular attention needs to be devoted to:

- the level and the nature of the fixed assets;
- the level of working capital – the difference between current assets and current liabilities;
- financing – the relative contributions from shareholders and lenders.

CHAPTER 7

The Cash Flow Statement in More Detail

INTRODUCTION

The purpose of this chapter is to emphasize the importance of good cash flow management and to show how to prepare and analyse a cash flow statement.

Looking at the profit and loss account and the balance sheet will confirm that it is not easy to identify the cash flowing into and out of a business. The profit and loss account includes transactions for which the cash settlement has not yet taken place, and it includes the depreciation charge, which is not a cash transaction at all. The balance sheet is a statement of assets and liabilities at a particular date. However, it includes some items that go back a number of years, such as fixed assets and share capital, and cash is only one of a number of items that receive attention.

A cash flow statement is, therefore, required which summarizes where cash came from and how it was spent. This is recognized by Financial Reporting Standard 1 (FRS1) on cash flow statements. It was published originally in September 1991 and revised in October 1996 so as to provide even clearer information on changes in cash and borrowings.

Cash flow statements explain the impact of operating, investment and financial transactions on a company's cash position between two balance sheet dates. Cash is the lifeblood of any business. Without cash, it cannot survive. It will be unable to meet its commitments such as salary payments at the end of the month and the repayments of borrowings. Such a situation provokes a crisis, for example the bank not being prepared to increase the overdraft facility or suppliers refusing to deliver raw materials because they have not been paid. In some cases, the crisis will deepen and mean that the business will be unable to carry on trading. As a result, liquidation may follow (not bankruptcy; that is for individuals). Therefore, the lack of cash is the equivalent of a heart attack – it is financial thrombosis. For all these reasons, we need to identify the sources from which cash can be generated and the uses to which it can be put. They are summarized in Figure 7.1.

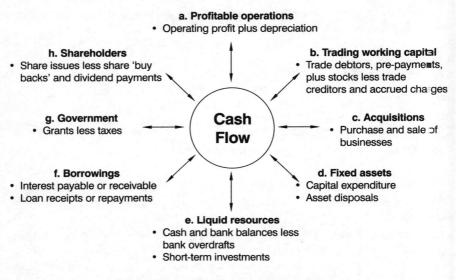

Figure 7.1   *Sources and uses of cash*

We will discuss each of the items in turn so that we can answer such questions as:

- To what extent was the business self-sufficient in cash terms?
- Did it need to rely on external finance?
- Did it meet its commitments from its own cash generation?
- To what extent have borrowings increased or fallen?
- How was the increase in working capital and capital expenditure financed?
- Did shareholders contribute additional share capital (a 'rights' issue)? If so, how much?

Note that all the arrows in the diagram indicate two-way flows. This indicates that items a–d and f–h may represent either sources or uses of cash. For example, item f, borrowings, will be a source of cash if loans increase during the financial period. However, if loans are repaid, cash will be used.

In the case of item e, liquid resources, these will rise if the other items overall result in a net source of cash. If the other items, overall, result in a net *use* of cash, then liquid resources will fall.

EXAMPLE

The Unilever Group's summarized cash flow statement for the year ended 31 December 1997 is described below to demonstrate the practical application of these various points.

	£m
Cash flow from operating activities	
Profitable operations	3,655
Reduction in working capital	203
	3,858
Capital expenditure	(875)
Acquisitions and business disposals	4,095
Taxation paid	(1,307)
Returns on investments and the servicing of finance	(237)
'Free' cash flow	5,534
Dividends paid to ordinary shareholders	(652)
Cash inflow/(outflow) before financing	**4,882**
Financing	
Reduction in borrowings	(476)
Increase in current investments such as cash on short-term deposit	(4,438)
	(4,914)
Reduction in cash at bank	32
	4,882

Cash flow from operating activities

Profitable operations

The potential generation of cash from operations is revenues less operating costs. However, operating costs usually include depreciation, which involves no payment of cash. So if we want to know the true potential impact of operating profit on cash, we should only include cash expenses. Therefore, the potential cash inflow is the sum of the operating profit plus the depreciation charge.

But this is not the end of the matter. The potential cash flow from trading activities will not result in cash that can be used for capital expenditure, debt repayments and dividends. This is because an allowance has to be made for credit transactions such as changes in trade debtors and creditors – the increases or decreases in working capital. Increases in working capital absorb cash such as additional stocks and extending credit to existing and new customers.

By contrast, increases in trade creditors – amounts due to suppliers – are, effectively, cash inflows since short-term commitments are not being immediately paid off.

Here are the Unilever Group's figures:

	£m
Operating profit	2,951
Add back depreciation	704
	3,655
Changes in working capital	
Reduction in stocks	84
Increase in debtors	(153)
Increase in creditors	272
	203
Cash flow from operating activities	3,858

As far as Unilever's working capital is concerned, there was actually a *reduction* in 1997 as a result of good, short-term asset management:

- Stock levels fell which released cash of £84 million.
- Trade creditors increased by £272 million – an effective *source* of cash.
- Trade debtors increased by £153 million – an effective *use* of cash.
- Overall, working capital fell by £203 million – a *net* source of cash.

Fixed assets (capital expenditure and asset disposals)

Unilever spent £957 million on capital expenditure offset by the cash it received from asset disposals of £82 million. This gives a net cash outflow of £875 million.

Acquisitions and the sale of businesses

Unilever acquired an ice cream company in Brazil for £919 million. However, this was more than offset by the sale of its speciality chemicals business to ICI for £4,562 million and other businesses for £452 million. Overall, this produced a net cash inflow of £4,095 million.

Taxation paid (£1,307 million)

This is the amount paid by Unilever for corporation tax both at home and abroad.

Returns on investments and the servicing of finance (£237 million)

This is a long-winded expression, which covers (a) interest payments less interest received and (b) dividends received from and paid to third parties such as preference shareholders.

'Free' cash flow

The cash flow from operating activities less capital expenditure, acquisitions, tax payments and net interest payments is sometimes referred to as 'free' cash flow. This is £5,534 million. The cash flow is 'free' in the sense that it is available to meet cash dividend payments to ordinary shareholders. Don't forget that ordinary shareholders are the owners of the business. Dividend payments are discretionary since they depend on the financial results that have been achieved.

Cash flow before financing

After deducting the dividends paid to ordinary shareholders of £652 million, the cash generated by the group was £4,882 million. This is called the cash inflow (or outflow) before financing because it is the cash generated or used up by the business without taking into consideration any changes in borrowings, share capital and opening cash balances.

If there is a cash surplus, as there is in the case of Unilever, the question is: what has the surplus been used for? If there is a cash deficit, the question is: how has the deficit been financed?

Financing

The financing section of the cash flow statement provides the answers. For Unilever, £476 million was used to reduce or repay borrowings, and £4,438 million was used for short-term investment purposes such as money market deposits. This totals £4,914 million. The difference between the financing uses of £4,914 million and the cash surplus of £4,882 million is £32 million, which is explained by a reduction of this amount in Unilever's cash at the bank.

CASH SELF-SUFFICIENCY

For any business, it is important to assess the extent to which it is self-sufficient in cash terms. This means the degree to which it is able to finance its operations and its capital investment programme, including acquisitions, without the need to rely on external financial support. There will be occasions where the demands of the business, such as a major new product development programme or a significant acquisition, will require additional funding from institutions and shareholders. But this cannot continue indefinitely since borrowings will become too high and shareholders will become reluctant to subscribe for additional capital as their investment becomes larger and their risk exposure increases. It is all a question of balance so that over, say, a five-year cycle, a company will be expected to be at least cash neutral – neither generating nor using up cash – to preserve its financial stability. For individual years, however, there may well be a cash surplus or a cash deficit according to the strategic requirements of the business.

Bass, for example, had negative cash flow before financing – a cash deficit of £148 million – in 1996 when there were relatively small asset disposals but significant capital expenditure and the acquisition of Carlsberg Tetley. In 1997, the situation reversed because there were large-scale asset and business disposals so that the cash flow before financing moved from a deficit to a surplus of £404 million.

The finance director of a major group such as BP or Coca-Cola will be concerned with the cash situation for the business as a whole. The perspective will be very wide-ranging. He or she will have to take account of all the different factors affecting cash flow including dividends, major acquisitions and tax payments. But for a business unit or subsidiary, which is part of a group of companies, the cash flow focus becomes narrower. The objective is to manage trading cash flows effectively since these are the cash flows over which local management has most control. Trading cash flow is usually defined as:

> The cash flow from operating activities (operating profit plus depreciation) plus or minus the change in working capital less capital expenditure.

For example, for the quarter ended 31 December 1998, Carling Sports, a subsidiary of Carling plc, achieved an operating profit of £1 million after deducting a depreciation charge of £100,000. The increase in working capital during the quarter was £250,000 and capital expenditure was £75,000.

	£000s
Operating profit	1,000
Add back depreciation	100
	1,100
Increase in working capital	(250)
Capital expenditure	(75)
Trading cash flow	**775**

By generating a positive cash flow, Carling Sports is contributing £775,000 to Carling plc's treasury. The business is not a cash drain. If the trading cash flow had been negative then Carling plc's treasury would have been obliged to support Carling Sports. This may have meant that Carling plc itself would have had to negotiate additional external financing. All of this means that accurate cash flow forecasting is essential – lenders and shareholders do not like surprises! For Carling plc its cash projections will only be as good as the individual forecasts of its constituent businesses. This means that great attention should be paid to trading cash flow.

SUMMARY

A satisfactory cash flow situation is essential if a business is to survive. If bills cannot be paid, if banks are refusing to agree to additional borrowing facilities, then a crisis will emerge which may be serious enough to threaten continuing viability. For all these reasons, a cash flow statement – especially a projected one – is a vital tool to guide a business so that potential problems can be anticipated rather than ignored.

The statement draws a distinction between cash flows from trading activities and cash flows from financing activities. Trading activities focus on profitable operations (adding back the depreciation charge), changes in working capital and the level of capital expenditure. Financing activities focus on contributions from shareholders, borrowings and the use of existing cash resources.

For an organization as a whole, the cash flow impact of both trading and financing activities will be of concern. At the business unit level, however, the focus will be on trading cash flows. Managing them successfully will help to ensure that the company, overall, controls its cash position effectively.

PART III

Financial Analysis

CHAPTER 8

The Analysis and Interpretation of Financial Statements

INTRODUCTION

In the earlier chapters, we concentrated on the significance of the profit and loss account, the balance sheet and the cash flow statement. The emphasis in this chapter will be different: we need to be able to interpret financial information, not just in terms of carrying out an 'inquest' – identifying those aspects of a business which are not in good financial shape – but also, and much more important, to use the numbers as the basis for performance improvement.

It is important to mention that the analysis of financial information involves the use of comparisons or ratios. A comment such as 'Marks & Spencer's operating profit was £1,116 million for the year ended 31 March 1998' is not particularly helpful. We do not know either the level of sales or capital employed required to achieve that result. And even if we did, we need to compare the results with other companies operating in the same business sector in order to assess Marks & Spencer's relative performance.

FINANCIAL OBJECTIVES

We need to be clear about the financial objectives of a business, which may be summarized as follows:

- To earn a superior and improving rate of return on capital employed (ROCE). This addresses the issues of profitability and the management of assets.

- To sustain a sound financial position. This addresses the issue of cash flow management – being able to meet short- and long-term commitments as they fall due.

The extent to which these objectives are being achieved can be judged by referring to four performance standards:

1. The expectations of investors who, in the case of publicly quoted companies, are large institutions such as insurance companies and pension funds.
2. The targets set by businesses internally in the form of budgets and longer-term financial plans.
3. The track record of the company concerned. Financial markets are not impressed by volatility – results that are relatively good one year and not at all good the next.
4. Competitors' performance. For example, is the business a top quartile performer by reference to its return on capital employed?

An example of a company that is taking these matters particularly seriously is BP (British Petroleum). In April 1998, it announced a set of millennium targets through to the year 2002. They include a 'strongly competitive' ROCE (at 17 per cent, BP's ROCE is currently the best in its peer group) and a commitment to keep its gearing below 30 per cent. The issue of gearing is discussed later in the chapter.

PROFITABILITY

The basic measure of profitability is the ROCE. ROCE is calculated by expressing 'profit' as a percentage of the capital employed to achieve that profit. For this purpose, profit is defined as operating or trading profit (profit before interest and taxation). Capital employed can be defined in a variety of ways. We shall use one of the most common definitions which is 'fixed assets plus current assets less current liabilities'. This is, of course, equal to fixed assets plus working capital or total assets less current liabilities. The use of this definition means that the figure for capital employed can be quickly identified from all balance sheets.

Essentially, the ROCE seeks to determine if the return generated by a company from its trading activities exceeds, or not, the return available to its lenders and shareholders from other comparable business opportunities. This return is referred to as the 'cost of capital' and is explained in more detail in Chapter 12. For example:

ROCE and the cost of capital (COC)

	ROCE %	COC %
Asda	14.0	11.2
J Sainsbury	9.0	10.4

Source: *The Sunday Times*, 27 September 1998

As you can see, Asda exceeded its cost of capital but J Sainsbury did not.

As you would expect, the average ROCE varies from business sector to business sector. For example, the 'Financial Times 500' published in January 1998, estimated that the average ROCE for advertising agencies was 28 per cent, for pharmaceutical companies 21 per cent, for chemical companies 15 per cent, and for car manufacturers 8 per cent.

The ROCE is influenced by two specific factors. The first is the profit margin and the second is asset turnover as explained below:

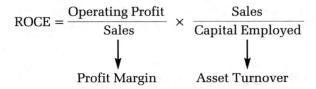

$$ROCE = \frac{\text{Operating Profit}}{\text{Sales}} \times \frac{\text{Sales}}{\text{Capital Employed}}$$

Profit Margin   Asset Turnover

Profit margin is defined as operating profit expressed as a percentage of sales. Asset turnover is defined as sales divided by capital employed expressed as a 'number of times'.

Profit margin focuses on the profitability of sales – for every £100 worth of sales, what is the level of operating profit? Asset turnover, by contrast, focuses on the extent to which fixed assets and working capital are being used to generate sales. It answers the question 'What level of sales has been generated for each pound or dollar of capital employed?' For example, the Coca-Cola company for the year ended 31 December 1997:

	$m
Operating profit	5,001
Sales	18,868
Capital employed	9,561

ROCE

$$\frac{\$5,001 \text{ million}}{\$18,868 \text{ million} \times 100\%} \times \frac{\$18,868 \text{ million}}{\$9,561 \text{ million}}$$

26.5%   1.97 times
Profit margin   Asset turnover

Source: Coca-Cola's 1997 Annual Report

Coca-Cola's ROCE equals 26.5 per cent × 1.97 which gives 52.2 per cent – not at all bad relative to other industries!

Capital intensive businesses such as oil exploration will have relatively low asset turnovers but relatively high profit margins. Industries that are less capital intensive such as advertising agencies will have relatively high asset turnovers but relatively low profit margins. For example, BP for the year ended 31 December 1997:

	Asset turnover	Profit margin	ROCE
Exploration and production	0.39 times	55.8%	21.8%
Oil refining and marketing	7.53 times	2.6%	19.6%

Source: BP's 1997 Annual Report

The important point to bear in mind, by separating out the two main influences on the ROCE, is that better asset management – an issue not obviously related to profitability – will lead to a higher ROCE even if profit margins cannot be sustained due, for example, to competitive pressures on selling prices.

Gross profit and the expense ratio

Two factors that have a particular influence on profit margins are the gross profit margin and the expense ratio.

Gross profit margins
As you may recall, the gross profit margin is the difference between sales and the cost of sales divided by sales expressed as a percentage. The cost of sales refers to the direct costs of the company's products and services such as materials and packaging. Therefore, the gross profit margin is a basic indicator of product profitability rather than the overall profitability of the business. For example, Unilever, year ended 31 December 1997:

	£m
Sales	29,766
Cost of sales	(16,477)
Gross profit	13,289

Source: Unilever's 1997 Annual Report

The gross profit margin is 44.6 per cent (£13,289 million divided by £29,766 million expressed as a percentage).

The overall gross profit margin is determined by the gross profit margins of individual products and services and the relative value of their sales. The greater the proportion of relatively high gross margin products, the higher the overall gross margin will be. The issue is one of managing the product or sales mix effectively.

It is important to bear in mind that very small changes to the overall gross profit margin will have a more than proportionate effect on overall profitability. For example, Marks & Spencer, year ended 31 March 1998:

	£m	£m
Sales	8,243	8,243
Cost of sales	(5,323)	(5,276)
Gross profit	2,920	2,967
Operating costs	(1,804)	(1,804)
Operating profit	1,116	1,163
Gross profit margin	35.4%	36%

Source: Marks & Spencer's 1998 Annual Report

The right-hand column shows a potential uplift in Marks & Spencer's gross margin from 35.4 per cent to 36 per cent; not on the face of it much of a change. However, this would produce an additional gross profit of £47 million which feeds straight through to a £47 million increase in operating profit – a rise of over 4 per cent for a 0.6 percentage point increase in gross margin.

The expense ratio

The expense ratio is calculated by expressing operating costs as a percentage of sales. In the case of Marks & Spencer, for example, for its 1997/98 financial year, it is £1,804 million divided by £8,243 million times 100 per cent, which works out at 21.9 per cent. The lower the expense ratio, the higher will be the level of operating profit. A combination of a higher gross profit margin and a lower expense ratio will be extremely good news for the bottom line!

For Marks & Spencer, a fall in the expense ratio from 21.9 per cent to, say, 21 per cent will produce an additional £73 million (or 6.5 per cent) of operating profit. This is because operating costs will fall from £1,804 million to £1,731 million.

Looking at both the gross profit margin and the expense ratio will help to identify problem areas. For example, if the operating profit margin is relatively low but the gross profit margin is relatively high, this may indicate that the expense ratio is too onerous, which may stimulate initiatives to improve cost competitiveness.

The return on equity (ROE)

This is a narrower definition than the ROCE since it looks at the perspective of shareholders only. It is calculated by taking the profit after taxation attributable to shareholders (the earnings) and expressing it as a percentage of the shareholders' equity. The significance of the ROE is that it highlights the return on the shareholders' investment only. For example, Marks & Spencer, year ended 31 March 1998:

	£m
Profit attributable to shareholders (earnings)	829
Shareholders' funds (equity)	5,066

ROE = £829 million ÷ £5,066 million × 100% = 16.4%

Source: Marks & Spencer's 1998 Annual Report

According to *The Economist* (29 August 1998) the average ROE for industrial companies in Europe is nearly 15 per cent.

FINANCIAL POSITION

So far, we have concentrated on the objective of profitability. But that is not the end of the story. Being profitable is necessary for a business but it is by no means sufficient. It needs to be in a sound financial position so that it can meet its short- and long-term commitments such as amounts due to suppliers and obligations to banks. The absence of a sound financial position will frustrate the ability of a company to sustain its profitability since it will not be able to invest in new capital equipment nor to increase its sales because lenders will be unwilling to finance extra working capital such as stocks.

There will tend to be a continual air of crisis, which will distract the management team since it will be preoccupied with difficult discussions with nervous bank managers and shareholders. Good cash flow is, therefore, essential and it is crucially important to focus on those indicators – the financial equivalents of blood pressure and pulse rate – that highlight cash flow performance. The starting point is both a short- and a longer-term cash flow forecast, which is simply a detailed estimate of expected cash receipts and payments with clear assumptions supporting the figures.

Ensuring a sound financial position is about managing the 'financing cycle' effectively. The cycle itself is shown in Figure 8.1. Imagine a start up situation for a company. In the first instance, it will obtain cash (box 3) from shareholders (the equity – circle 1) and lenders (debt – circle 2). As the business starts to trade, it will interact with suppliers (trade creditors – box 5) so that it can purchase raw materials and services (box 6). The raw materials will be converted to work in progress (box 7) and then turned into finished goods (box 8). With some delay, the finished goods and services will be sold (box 9). At this stage, the sales will not produce cash because customers (the trade debtors – box 10) will not pay until several weeks after they have received the sales invoice. Thus, there will be a further delay between boxes 10 and 3 which is the time it takes for trade debtors to settle their bills and to 'top up' the cash 'tank' in box 3.

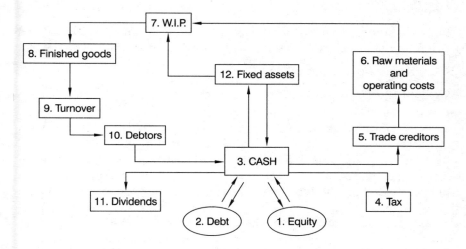

Figure 8.1   *Financing cycle*

The level of the cash 'tank' will be affected also by the level of capital expenditure (offset by asset disposals – box 12) and the payment of dividends (box 11) and tax (box 4). To the extent that the level of cash in the 'tank' is too low, it will need to be 'topped up', particularly by increases in short-term debt which will flow from box 2 to box 3.

Boxes 1 and 2 (as well as 12) show two-way flows. Equity can be received (box 2) from shareholders and returned to them by share 'buy backs'. Likewise, debt can be increased in the form of extra borrowings and reduced by loan repayments. Fixed assets (box 12) can be purchased and they can be sold.

There is another important point about the financing cycle: interdependence. For example, if the delay in receiving cash (between boxes 10 and 3) is increasing, then the level of cash in the 'tank' will fall. It will have to be topped up from other sources (such as debt – box 2) if the business is to continue to trade. Similarly, if there is a build-up in finished goods (box 8), this will lead to lower sales, lower debtors and lower levels of cash received. Again, the cash 'tank' will need to be topped up. If the situation becomes particularly serious, then capital expenditure may have to be postponed or cancelled and new financing arrangements may have to be negotiated. Therefore, the objective of achieving a sound financial position will only be possible by managing the financing cycle effectively. To help us to do so, there are a number of important indicators, which are explained below.

Liquidity

Liquidity focuses on the ability of a business to meet its short-term commitments – those falling due within one year of the balance sheet date.

Stock turnover rate
Stock levels, covering raw materials, work in progress and finished goods, should be minimized subject, of course, to maintaining competitive levels of customer service. This is because resources tied up in stocks are extremely expensive; for example, the interest charges on the cash used to finance the stocks, the costs of storage, warehousing and insurance and the risks of being left with stock that cannot be sold due to deterioration, obsolescence and changes in customer requirements. It has been esti-mated that the annual total of stock holding costs comes to between 15 and 20 per cent of the average stock value. For example, Marks & Spencer's stocks at the end of March 1998 were valued at £500 million. It is costing the company £75–100 million a year to manage them.

The indicator measuring the effectiveness of stock management is called the stock turnover rate. This is the average number of times each year that stocks are 'turned over'. It is calculated by dividing the cost of sales by the average or closing stocks. When the ratio is computed from published information, the cost of sales figure may not be given. Even if it is, the definition of the cost of sales varies from company to company and it may include items such as depreciation which have nothing to do with stock at all. For this reason, an alternative definition is used which is sales divided by the average or closing stock. For example, Marks & Spencer, year ended 31 March 1998:

	£m	
Sales	8,243	(A)
Year end stocks	500	(B)

(A) ÷ (B) = 16.5 times

Source: Marks & Spencer's 1998 Annual Report

This means that, on average, an item of stock is either on the shelves, in a store, in transit or in a warehouse for 3.15 weeks (52 weeks divided by 16.5).

As with the gross profit margin, the stock turnover rate can not only be calculated for a business as a whole but also for individual products. This means that stock problems can be identified at an early stage, particularly by monitoring the stock turnover rates at regular intervals to discern the underlying trends. One point is clear: a steadily reducing stock turnover rate is a clear sign of problems ahead. Cash flow difficulties may be on the horizon.

Stock turnover rates differ from industry to industry. They tend to be relatively low in manufacturing companies (5–10 times) and relatively high in retailing and contracting (15–20 times).

Collection period

This is the average length of time taken by customers to pay their sales invoices. It is calculated by dividing trade debtors (not total debtors) by annual sales and multiplying the result by 365 days to give the average number of days for which sales invoices have been outstanding. For example, Unilever, year ended 31 December 1997:

	£m	
Trade debtors	2,545	(A)
Sales	29,766	(B)

The collection period is:
(A) ÷ (B) × 365 days = 31 days

Source: Unilever's 1997 Annual Report

The collection period is a measure of the effectiveness of a company's credit control system. The shorter the collection period, the better the credit control. If the terms of business indicate a collection period of 45 days and it is actually 60 days, there is a problem to be sorted out.

It is possible to carry out a more detailed analysis of the overall collection period by looking at the amounts owed by each customer and the length of time for which they have been outstanding. This is called an aged debtor analysis and it will pinpoint overdue amounts, which can then be chased and collected. Common sense suggests that the longer the collection period, the less chance there will be that the amount owed by the customer will be collected in full. This means that bad debt provisions may need to be considered. The effect is to reduce the value of the trade debtor by the amount of the provision and to charge the provision as an additional cost in the profit and loss account. Bad debt provisions, therefore, have an adverse impact both on cash flow and on profitability. Most companies have a standard procedure that applies bad debt provisions on a rising scale according to the length of time for which the total amount outstanding has been overdue.

The collection period should be compared to the credit period granted by suppliers. This is calculated by dividing trade creditors plus accrued charges by the value of the purchases of goods and services and multiplying the result by 365 days. Such information is very difficult to find from published sources. However, one way of overcoming the problem is to express both trade debtors and trade creditors plus accrued charges as a percentage of sales. If trade debtors are 25 per cent of sales and trade creditors plus accrued charges are only 15 per cent of sales, it indicates that suppliers are being paid before cash is received from customers. This is a situation to avoid since there is a financing gap that will have to be bridged by relying on short-term borrowings such as a bank overdraft.

The current ratio and the acid-test ratio

These are the two ratios that are often used in assessing a company's overall liquidity (its ability to meet its short-term commitments). However, they do need to be used with care since different industries have different norms and it is the trends in the ratios that are of particular significance.

Both ratios focus on a company's current assets (stocks, debtors and cash balances) and its current liabilities (accrued charges, trade creditors and bank overdrafts).

Current ratio = Current assets divided by current liabilities
Quick or 'acid-test' ratio = Current assets less stocks divided by current liabilities

For example, Marks & Spencer at 31 March 1998:

	£m
Current assets (including stocks)	3,403
Stocks	500
Current liabilities	2,345

Current ratio: £3,403 million ÷ £2,345 million = 1.45 : 1
Quick ratio: (£3,403 – £500 million) ÷ £2,345 million = 1.24 : 1

Source: Marks & Spencer's 1998 Annual Report

The current ratio is a general indicator of Marks & Spencer's short-term financial position. Its ratio of more than one indicates a surplus of current assets over current liabilities. A current ratio of two or more used to be regarded as prudent, but a figure of about 1.00 to 1.50:1 has become normal. A higher figure is not necessarily a good sign since it may be due to excessive stocks, debtors and cash balances which could be more profitably invested. There are no straightforward guidelines about what a company's current ratio ought to be. It depends on a number of factors such as:

- the nature of the company's business;
- the nature of the current assets (some may be very difficult to dispose of such as work in progress);
- the repayment dates of the current liabilities – if a loan is due for repayment very early in the financial year, this may be problematical especially if there is limited scope for further borrowings because the bank will not increase the overdraft facility;
- the seasonality of the working capital requirement.

It is important to note that not all current assets may be readily convertible into cash, especially stocks. This is highlighted by the 'quick' ratio. It excludes stocks from current assets and applies the 'acid' test of what would happen if a company had to pay its short-term creditors without delay. If the 'quick' ratio is less than one, it would be unable to do so. However, some companies such as supermarkets have terms of trade so that they sell goods for cash before paying for them. For example, J Sainsbury's 'quick' ratio at the end of its 1997/1998 financial year was only 0.52.

The working capital to sales ratio
Working capital – current assets less current liabilities – tends to rise as sales increase. Trading working capital (which is defined as stocks plus trade debtors less trade creditors plus accrued charges) expressed as a percentage of sales indicates how much working capital is required to finance the business, quite apart from the cash needed for capital expenditure. For example, Hatton Ltd is preparing its 1999 budget. The draft figures are as follows:

	Actual results in 1998 (£m)	Budget for 1999 (£m)
Sales	50	60
Trading working capital	10	12
The working capital to sales ratio	20%	20%

The company requires an additional £2 million of working capital so that sales can increase by 20 per cent from £50 million in 1998 to a projected £60 million in 1999. The extra working capital needs to be financed – extra cash and/or short-term borrowings of £2 million will be required. This amount can be reduced by better working capital management, for example, by reducing stocks and trade debtors. If Hatton Ltd's working capital to sales ratio could be reduced from 20 per cent to 17.5 per cent, then its working capital requirement in 1999 would be £10.5 million (17.5 per cent × the budgeted sales of £60 million). This means that its additional cash requirement will be £500,000 rather than £2 million.

A company that regards efficient working capital management as a particular priority is General Electric (GE) in the USA. Over the five years to the end of 1997, its investment in working capital has fallen from 20 per cent to 13.5 per cent of sales.

Solvency

Solvency focuses on the ability of a business to meet its longer-term commitments – those commitments that have to be met at least 12 months after the balance sheet date. The terminology is a bit confusing because a company is described as being insolvent if it is unable to meet its obligations as and when they fall due. Such a situation will precipitate a short-term crisis, which, if it is not sorted out, will mean that the company concerned may not survive to enjoy the longer term!

There are two principal indicators of solvency. The first is concerned with gearing or the extent to which both short- and long-term borrowings are a feature of a company's financing arrangements. The second is the interest cover which is a measure of the extent to which interest charges or financing costs affect overall profitability.

Gearing

There are many different definitions. However, the one used by investment analysts when they comment on a company's financial position is the debt-equity ratio. Debt is the net debt, which is the sum of the short- and long-term borrowings (including lease obligations) less liquid resources (cash balances and short-term investments). Equity is the shareholders' interest or the share capital and reserves. The purpose of the ratio is to measure the burden of debt (the external finance) in relation to the capital provided by shareholders (the internal finance). The higher the debt burden, the more onerous will be the level of interest charges and the debt repayment schedules. The risk to shareholders will also increase. For example, BP as at 31 March 1998:

	£m
Liquid resources	311
Short-term borrowings	1,749
Long-term borrowings	2,908
Shareholders' equity	14,095

The debt equity ratio is:

$$\frac{(£1,749 \text{ million} + £2,908 \text{ million} - £311 \text{ million})}{(£14,095 \text{ million})} \times 100\% = 31\%$$

Source: BP's first quarter results, 1998

As with the current and 'quick' ratios, there are no particular rules of thumb about what is a good and what is a bad debt-equity ratio. But financial commentators suggest that debt-equity ratios above 50 per cent do need to be justified. Debt-equity ratios above 100 per cent place a special challenge on a company but they are not unknown, for example among airlines.

A variation on the debt-equity ratio is the debt to the debt plus equity ratio. This definition looks at the proportion of debt in relation to the total financing of a business rather than just the equity element. In this case, the total debt is the gross debt – short- and long-term borrowings without deducting liquid resources. For example, BP as at 31 March 1998:

	£m
Short-term borrowings	1,749
Long-term borrowings	2,908
Equity	14,095

The debt to the debt plus equity ratio is:

$$\frac{(£1,749 \text{ million} + £2,908 \text{ million})}{(£1,749 \text{ million} + £2,908 \text{ million} + £14,095 \text{ million})} \times 100\% = 25\%$$

Source: BP's first quarter results, 1998

In April 1998, BP announced that, on this definition, its target gearing ratio is below 30 per cent for the period up to the year 2002.

Interest cover
The interest cover expresses the operating or trading profit, the profit before interest charges and taxation, as a multiple of the interest charge. It is a measure of the extent to which the operating profit covers the interest charge. For example, BAA, year ended 31 March 1998:

	£m	
Operating profit	521	(A)
Net interest charges (interest payable less interest receivable)	118	(B)

Interest cover = (A) ÷ (B) = 4.4 times

Source: BAA's 1998 Annual Report

According to the Lex Column in *The Financial Times* (10 August 1998), the average interest cover in the past for UK companies has been five times.

In extreme cases, a high debt to equity or gearing ratio may result in a significant interest charge, which may reduce or even remove the profit before taxation. For example, Gubbins Ltd, year ended 31 January 1999:

	£m
Operating profit	20
Interest charges	(21)
Loss before taxation	1

In this case, the financing burden is so great that the interest cover is less than 1. Although the company is profitable at the operating level, it falls into loss after the deduction of interest charges.

One other important aspect of the interest cover is that lenders may stipulate a level below which it should not fall (normally three or four times) as one of the conditions in a formal loan agreement.

Debt maturity profile

Quite apart from gearing, another factor which is important in assessing a company's ability to service its borrowings is the maturity profile of its debt obligations. In simple language, this means, when do the borrowings fall due for repayment and, in particular, what proportion of the debt is short term and what proportion is long term? The issue is straightforward – the greater the proportion of short-term debt in relation to total debt, the less flexibility a company has in meeting its commitments since the bulk of the repayments are due within a year. However, if the proportion of short-term debt is relatively low (say 20–30 per cent), then there is much more room for manoeuvre since the repayments fall later and there is less time pressure if borrowing arrangements need to be renegotiated. For example, BP as at 31 March 1998:

	£m
Short-term borrowings	1,749
Long-term borrowings	2,908
Total borrowings	4,657

Short-term borrowings as a percentage of total borrowings = 38 per cent

Source: BP's first quarter results, 1998

Credit ratings

There are two main credit rating agencies: Standard and Poors (S & P) and Moodies. The US Government has the highest rating AAA+ from S & P and Aaa1 from Moodies. The ratings are arranged on a sliding scale from AAA+ down to BB or below for 'junk bonds'. The ratings themselves depend to a significant extent on a company's level of gearing. The credit ratings a company receives directly determine the interest rate on its borrowings. For example, a company with an AAA–rating will be charged a lower interest rate than a company with an AA–rating. If the borrowings concerned are in billions of pounds (as in the case of BP), then very small differences in interest rates such as 0.05 per cent or 0.10 per cent will produce large savings in financing costs.

SUMMARY OF FINANCIAL PERFORMANCE INDICATORS

We have covered a number of indicators of profitability and financial position and they are summarized below:

- **Profitability**
  ROCE – the return on capital employed;
  profit margin;
  asset turnover;
  gross profit margin;
  expense ratio;
  return on equity.

- **Financial position**
  Liquidity:
  stock turnover rate;
  collection period;
  current ratio;
  quick ratio;
  working capital to sales ratio.

  Solvency:
  debt-equity ratio;
  debt to debt plus equity ratio;
  interest cover.

PERFORMANCE IMPROVEMENT PLAN

Working out the indicators is the first stage. If this can be done for a number of financial periods to identify trends, and against competitors to assess relative performance, then so much the better.

The second stage is to draw practical conclusions as the basis for performance improvement. An example is given below.

St Giles Limited
Profitability
- The ROCE has averaged 15 per cent over the past three years. This is a bottom quartile performance compared with 'best practice' competitors who have achieved 25 per cent.

- Profit margins versus competitors have been satisfactory at 15 per cent. However, asset turnover at 1.00 times has been somewhat lower than competitors who achieved 1.65 times.
- Gross margins have fallen from 50 per cent to 40 per cent since 1996.
- The expense ratio has been unchanged at 25 per cent since 1996.

Financial position
Liquidity
- The stock turnover rate is 4 times (somewhat lower than the best competitors at 6 times).
- The collection period is 90 days compared with 75 days 12 months ago.
- The working capital to sales ratio is 40 per cent (best practice competitors achieved 20 per cent).

Solvency
- The debt-equity ratio at 35 per cent is perfectly satisfactory.
- The interest cover at 6 times is 'safe'.

The third stage is to prepare a performance improvement plan, which is discussed below.

The use of financial performance measures by themselves does not indicate their direct influence on the ROCE. This can be achieved by preparing a Du Pont diagram or a 'pyramid' of figures as shown in Figure 8.2.

We have seen already that the ROCE is 15 per cent; the diagram indicates how it has been achieved. The profit before interest and taxation (PBIT) of £15 million is based on revenues of £100 million and total costs of £85 million. The revenues of £100 million are split between two products: A with revenues of £60 million, and B with revenues of £40 million. The costs of £85 million can be broken down into the direct costs of £60 million (for example, labour and materials) and operating costs of £25 million (such as advertising, salaries and utility charges).

The capital employed of £100 million consists of the fixed assets of £60 million and the trading working capital of £40 million. The fixed assets themselves can be split between the buildings of £40 million and the plant and equipment of £20 million. Similarly, the working capital consists of the trade debtors of £25 million, the stock of £25 million, less the trade creditors of £10 million to give £40 million.

The task is to identify those factors that have the most effect on the ROCE and to consider what can be done to manage them more effectively. For example, the working capital to sales ratio at 40 per cent is double that of 'best practice' competitors. What can be done to reduce it?

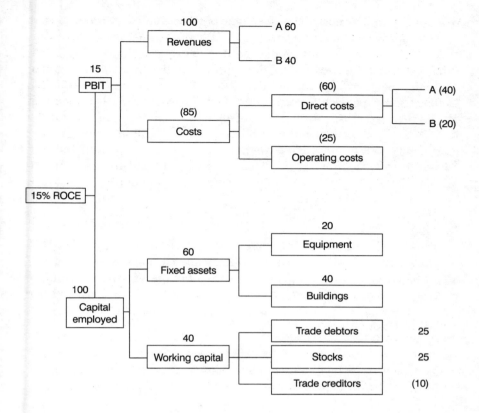

Figure 8.2   *St Giles Limited. Factors affecting the return on capital employed (£m)*

For a start, trade debtors are 25 per cent of sales whereas trade creditors are only 10 per cent. This means that suppliers are being paid before cash is received from customers. If trade debtors could be reduced to 20 per cent of sales and trade creditors increased to 15 per cent of sales over a six-month period, then £10 million of working capital would be released (trade debtors down by £5 million and trade creditors up by £5 million). If the stock turnover rate could be increased from four times (sales of £100 million divided by stocks of £25 million) to, say, five times, then a further £5 million reduction in working capital would occur so that the total reduction would be £15 million. The working capital to sales ratio would then be 25 per cent rather than 40 per cent, a significant step in the right direction.

Similar principles can be applied to the fixed assets. The buildings are two-thirds of the total fixed assets. If there is surplus accommodation, for example, it may be possible to sell some of the buildings to produce cash and to improve the asset turnover.

As far as the profit and loss account is concerned, there is scope for improvement even though St Giles' profit margins are competitive. For example, the gross profit margin is under pressure because it has fallen from 50 to 40 per cent over the last three years. You will notice that product A has a gross profit margin of 33.33 per cent (sales of £60 million less direct costs of £40 million divided by £60 million times 100 per cent). However, product B's gross profit margin is 50 per cent (sales of £40 million less direct costs of £20 million divided by sales of £40 million times 100 per cent). Even if overall sales cannot be increased it makes sense to try to alter the product mix so that a higher proportion of B is sold, since this will improve the total gross margin and benefit the ROCE.

In practice, a variety of initiatives will contribute to a greater ROCE. The value of the Du Pont diagram (which can be prepared in the form of a spreadsheet) is that the effect of a change in a particular factor on the ROCE can be calculated so that a comprehensive performance improvement plan can be prepared. It involves a five-step process, shown in Figure 8.3.

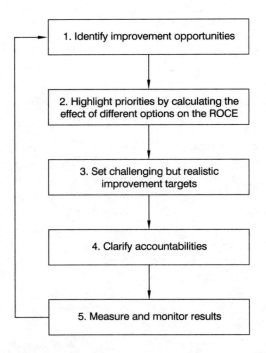

Figure 8.3   *Performance improvement plan*

SUMMARY

There are two principal financial objectives: the first is to be profitable, the second is to be in a sound financial position.

Profitability is measured by the return on capital employed (ROCE). Being in a sound financial position (or not) is measured by a variety of indicators such as the current ratio, the debt-equity ratio and interest cover.

All of these measures are relative; they need to be assessed against a number of benchmarks. These include the expectations of investors, internal targets, track record and performance versus competitors.

To use the indicators as a basis for achieving improved results, a three-stage approach is required. First, the indicators need to be calculated over several financial periods to identify the trends. Second, conclusions need to be drawn from the analysis. Third, a performance improvement plan needs to be developed using a Du Pont diagram as a financial model of a business. The diagram enables the effect of different factors on the ROCE to be worked out so that priorities can be determined and action taken.

CHAPTER 9

Investors' Performance Measures

INTRODUCTION

Investors, the owners of private and publicly quoted businesses, are interested in the actual and potential return achieved by the companies in their investment portfolios. In the case of quoted companies, shareholders are usually large financial institutions such as insurance companies, unit trusts and pension funds. These organizations account, for example, for 83 per cent of the ownership of BAA's shares. Private individuals account for the remaining 17 per cent.

The purpose of this chapter is to explain the indicators used by investors in their financial assessment of a business.

SHAREHOLDER RETURN

Shareholder return is influenced by a number of factors, which are discussed in more detail later in this chapter. It is the wealth returned to a shareholder over a specific period and is calculated by adding the rise (or fall) in the share price to the dividends per share actually received and expressing the result as a percentage of the opening share price. The return is normally expressed on a pre-tax or gross basis so that it can be compared more easily with the returns available from other investment opportunities. For example, BAA plc, financial year ended 31 March 1998:

Share price, 31 March 1998   583p
Share price, 1 April 1997   514p

Dividends paid:

19 August 1997 (final dividend)	7.9p
23 January 1998 (interim dividend)	4.9p
	12.8p

Shareholder return:

$$\frac{(583p - 514p) + 12.8p}{514p} \times 100\% = 15.9\%$$

Note that BAA's final dividend was based on its results for the year ended 31 March 1997. Its interim dividend was based on its results for the first half of its 1997/1998 financial year, which ended on 30 September 1997.

According to *The Economist* (29 August 1998) and based on a survey of 400 British companies carried out by the PA Consulting Group, shareholder return has varied between 5 and 17 per cent annually.

The factors influencing shareholder return

There are two key influences on shareholder return: the growth in earnings per share, and cash generation.

Earnings per share (EPS)

As we saw earlier, this is the profit after taxation attributable to ordinary shareholders divided by the number of issued ordinary shares. Consistent growth in EPS is a fundamental financial objective since it is concerned with the extent to which improved levels of profitability have been sustained over several years. The quality of the earnings growth is especially important if a company is to maintain its reputation in the financial markets. This means that investors look for continual growth in EPS rather than a 'flash in the pan' type of performance. They do not like surprises! In August 1998, for example, there was comment in *The Financial Times* about Rentokil Initial, since it was the first time in 13 years that it had failed to achieve its target of 20 per cent annual growth in earnings per share.

Earnings per share can be increased by share buy-backs, which means that companies purchase their own shares in the market thus reducing the number of shares in issue. For a given level of earnings, therefore, earnings per share will rise. *The Financial Times* reported (23 July 1998) that, since 1990, about 70 per cent of all European share buy-backs had taken place in the UK. A number of leading companies such as BT, BG (part of what was British Gas) and GEC have already purchased a proportion of their shares or have announced plans to do so. Share buy-backs are also widespread in the USA.

Cash generation
We have talked about cash flow in earlier chapters. From an investor's point of view, positive and improving cash flows allow higher dividends to be paid. They also provide the financial 'muscle' to facilitate higher levels of capital expenditure, which helps to secure the future of a business in existing and new markets.

Growth in EPS and cash generation have an important influence on a number of other measures which are of considerable interest to investors.

MARKET CAPITALIZATION

This is the value placed upon a company's equity or ordinary shares. It is calculated by multiplying the number of issued ordinary shares by the market price per share. For example, BAA plc at 31 March 1998:

Number of issued ordinary shares 1,055,585,691 (rather a lot!)   (A)
Share price 582.5p   (B)
Market capitalization (A) × (B) = £6.15 billion

On 31 August 1998, the UK's largest company in terms of market capitalization was Glaxo Wellcome (£64.8 billion). At the beginning of August 1998, the world's three largest companies in terms of market capitalization were:

	£bn
General Electric (USA)	106
Microsoft	96
Coca-Cola	73

BOOK VALUE PER SHARE

This is the asset backing supporting each ordinary share based upon the 'valuations', principally historic cost, in the balance sheet. The greater the asset backing, the more the current share price can be justified, even if the earnings prospects are not attractive.

The book value per share is calculated by dividing the shareholders' equity, as shown in the balance sheet (the 'book' value) by the number of issued ordinary shares. For example, BAA plc at 31 March 1998:

(A) Shareholders' equity, £3,739 million
(B) Number of ordinary shares, 1,055,585,691
Book value per share = (A) ÷ (B) = £3.54

A company's stock market value divided by its book value is called the 'market to book' ratio. The higher the 'market to book' ratio, the greater the financial standing a company has among investors because its reputation is based not upon its assets but its earning power and intangible factors such as its brand image and the quality of its 'top' management team. Coca-Cola, for example, had a market to book ratio of 10 times at the beginning of August 1998. By comparison, BTR, the British engineering group, whose future is uncertain, had a market to book ratio of only 0.6. Relatively low market to book ratios make a company vulnerable to being taken over, as the publisher Cassell discovered in October 1998 when it received a hostile bid from Macmillan. At the time, Cassell's 'market to book' ratio was about 0.7.

Here is an example of a 'market to book' calculation – BP as at 30 June 1998:

(A) Market capitalization   £44,079 million
(B) Book value of shareholders' equity   £14,354 million
Market to book ratio = (A) ÷ (B) = 3.07

PRICE/EARNINGS RATIO (P/E RATIO)

It is not appropriate to compare the EPS in one company with that of another since the size of the companies and the number of shares issued vary widely. The p/e ratio is a way of comparing the stock market's assessment of different companies since it is regarded as a kind of financial status symbol. It is calculated by dividing the latest market price of a particular share by the latest annual earnings per share to give the number of years' earnings represented by the current share price. The p/e ratio is also referred to as 'the earnings multiple'. For example, BAA plc:

Share price as at 3 September 1998   605p   (A)
Latest annual earnings per share   36.4p   (B)
p/e ratio = (A) ÷ (B) = 16.6 times

It is the relative size of the p/e ratio which is important. The absolute figure is not very meaningful. In early September 1998, the average p/e ratio for the FT 'top 100' companies by market capitalization was 19.6. The higher the p/e ratio, the more attractive a company's prospects are perceived to be, especially the outlook for earnings growth. By contrast, the lower the p/e ratio, the less favourable the market view about the earnings outlook. These views are, however, based on perceptions and the facts may be somewhat different. The challenge is to discover companies with low p/e ratios but with excellent earnings prospects!

The average p/e ratio will also vary from business sector to business sector according to the market view about the sector's prospects. For example, in early September 1998, BTR had a p/e ratio of only 8.5. By contrast, Zeneca, a leading pharmaceutical company, had a p/e ratio of 28.4. On a business sector basis, engineering had an average p/e ratio of only 11.4, whereas property had an average p/e ratio of 21.7.

The historic p/e ratio is based on the latest reported earnings per share. The forward or prospective p/e ratio is based on the forecast earnings per share over the next 12 months. If this prospective p/e ratio is regarded as being too low, then there is a possibility that the share price will be upgraded to produce a higher p/e ratio.

DIVIDEND YIELD

This is the annual dividend per share, before tax, expressed as a percentage of the share price. For example, Marks & Spencer:

Annual dividend per share in 1997/98	17.9p	(A)
Share price at 3 September 1998	532p	(B)

Dividend yield = (A) ÷ (B) × 100% = 3.4%

Again, the dividend yield is a comparative measure. A relatively low dividend yield implies that an investor is prepared to accept a small dividend income today. But the expectation is that the share price will rise since earnings prospects are regarded as being good. The prospect of an appreciation in the share price is compensation for the relatively low dividend income.

A relatively high dividend yield implies that an investor is not prepared to wait for an appreciation in the share price because the outlook for earnings growth is regarded as unattractive and/or the risk of holding the company's shares is seen to be high. An investor wants a relatively high dividend income as compensation for the uncertain future prospects.

The average dividend yield for companies in the FT 'top 100' by market capitalization was 3.3 per cent in early September 1998. BTR's dividend yield was 7.4 per cent. But Rentokil Initial's was only 1.2 per cent – optimism remains about its earnings growth prospects.

DIVIDEND COVER

This is calculated by dividing a company's earnings by its dividend or its earnings per share by its dividend per share. For example, Marks & Spencer:

Earnings for the year ended 31 March 1998   £829 million   (A)
Dividend for the same period   £409 million   (B)
Dividend cover = (A) ÷ (B) = 2.03 times

The significance of the dividend cover is that it is a measure of the security of the dividend, since it focuses on the number of times that the earnings are greater than the dividend. The higher the dividend cover, the more secure the dividend since, if earnings fall, the less likely it will be that the dividend will also fall. The average dividend cover for UK companies is about 2 and some businesses such as GEC have announced that it is their intention to achieve a specific cover. In the case of GEC it also happens to be 2.

An uncovered dividend means that the dividend cover is less than 1 since dividends are greater than earnings. Such a situation may lead to future dividends being reduced or 'passed' – no dividend at all may be paid.

A variation on the dividend cover is the payout ratio. This is the annual dividend expressed as a percentage of earnings. For example, a dividend cover of 2 is equivalent to a payout ratio of 50 per cent.

SUMMARY

Investors are preoccupied with shareholder return. The two principal factors affecting 'shareholder return' performance are earnings per share and cash generation. There are also a number of other measures which investors focus on and they include market capitalization, book value per share, the price/earnings ratio, dividend yield and dividend cover. All of these indicators will be affected by the earnings outlook and the cash flow situation.

Management Accounting

The Use of Management Accounting Information for Decision-making Purposes

INTRODUCTION

The correct analysis and interpretation of management accounting information is an essential ingredient in good decision making. One of the main keys to interpretation is understanding the behaviour of revenues and costs. For example: how do costs change if the level of activity changes? What level of activity is required to earn a profit? Which product or product line is the most profitable?

The purpose of this chapter is to explore such issues.

COSTS

First, we will look at costs, with a focus on:

- cash, non-cash and non-financial costs;
- relevant costs for decision making –
  differential, incremental and avoidable costs
  sunk costs
  opportunity costs;
- break-even analysis, fixed and variable costs;
- contribution and marginal cost;
- the importance of cost structure;
- key factor analysis.

Cost – a definition

The definition of what 'cost' is depends on who you are talking to. To an accountant, cost is a monetary measurement of the amount of resources used for some purpose. To an economist, the term 'cost' may have a broader meaning. It is characterized by the idea of sacrifice. Not all sacrifices involve using resources; some involve wasting an opportunity, on which the economist will seek to place a value. Both these approaches are relevant in decision making.

Cash, non-cash and non-financial costs

Cash and deferred cash costs are those reflected in actual cash outflows. The outflow may be immediate, such as when urgently needed office supplies are bought with petty cash. Alternatively, the outflow may be later as when raw materials are purchased on credit. The cost to the company is based on the monetary value of the resource made available; it is recognized as the resource is used.

Non-cash costs result from the recognition that a resource is being used up or is wearing out. The most common example of this concept is depreciation. Another example of a non-cash cost is an opportunity cost.

Non-financial costs are costs that are not directly traceable through a company's accounts. While such costs may lead indirectly to a reduced cash flow in the future, they do not represent any expenditure. Examples are the costs associated with a loss of company image if it causes pollution, or is convicted of unfair trading. There is no financial value that can be recorded for such 'costs'.

Although the traditional accountant may not be able to recognize non-financial costs, the economist and management accountant may well try to measure their economic impact.

Differential, incremental and avoidable costs

Differential and incremental costs are different terms with the same or very similar meanings.

Differential costs are the changes in overall cost that occur between options. Suppose an engineer wants to requisition replacements for a pump and for a valve. Both items can be provided by either of two companies, at the following prices:

	Pump £	Valve £
Company A	195	270
Company B	195	285

It is clear that the economics of the decision about which company to go to depend on the valve prices. These are the differential costs of the decision.

In this simple example, it is easy to discriminate between the differential and other unchanging costs. In reality, considerable analysis may be needed to identify them, as we shall see. However, the basic principle – that the economic decision is determined by differential costs – remains unchanged.

The idea of incremental costs uses exactly the same approach of identifying the extra costs implicit in a decision. It is a term often met, for example, in investment appraisal (see Chapter 12). If a facility is to be extended, we want to compare the investment in the extension with the incremental costs, revenues or savings that will result, over and above the costs and revenues that would flow from the facility if unaltered.

Avoidable costs represent another way of viewing the same costs from a different standpoint. In choosing whether to continue operating as at present or whether to use an alternative approach, we can avoid some existing costs if we switch to the alternative. It is how the option's costs compare with the avoidable costs that is important. Costs continuing in any event, that are unavoidable, are irrelevant to the economic decision. Here is an example:

The Slithy Toves and Mome Raths Co-operative has a special machine for producing borogroves. It is located in a machine shop, which has no lack of space and, as there are several workers who can set up and operate the machine, it has been made a cost centre. The annual sales budget for borogroves has been set at 100 per week; the machine's capacity is 150 per week.

The cost accountant has set the cost of a borogrove at £14.50. This she breaks down into:

	£
Material	9.73
Direct labour	2.35
Overhead recovery	2.42
	14.50

The overhead recovery may be analysed as follows:

	£
Supervision	56.00
Depreciation*	48.00
Test and inspection section	37.00
Contract maintenance charge*	10.00
General factory overhead	91.00
	242.00

*Both of these charges result from the special machine. The first is the cost of the machine's depreciation; the second is the cost of an annual contract for its specialist maintenance.

Divided at the budgeted weekly rate of 100 borogroves, this equals £2.42 for each borogrove.

Questions

The company's sales manager says that he has an opportunity to sell another 10 borogroves a week into a new market segment at a price of £13.50 each. He seeks your approval to accept the additional business at this price. What is your decision?

The variable cost of making a borogrove is £12.08. This is the material cost of £9.73 plus the direct labour cost of £2.35. The new market segment's selling price is £13.50. Therefore, the additional business should be accepted provided that the selling of extra units at £13.50 each does not have an adverse impact on the pricing situation in the co-operative's existing markets.

Later, a representative from another borogrove manufacturer calls at your office. He offers to sell you all the borogroves you need at a price of £13.00 each. Should you accept the offer? Should you make or buy?

The direct cost of making a borogrove – the costs that will not be incurred if the borogroves are bought – are the variable costs of £12.08 plus the direct overhead costs (depreciation of £48 plus contract maintenance of £10 which works out at £58 for 100 borogroves or 58p for each one). The total 'make' cost is, therefore, £12.66. The saving on making is £13.00 less £12.66, which is 34p for each borogrove. The cash saving on making is £13 less £12.18, which equals 82p for each borogrove. £12.18 is the £12.08 plus the 10p for the contract maintenance.

Sunk costs

The sunk cost idea is really an application of the differential cost principle. It requires managers to recognize that costs already incurred cannot be recovered, and are, therefore, irrelevant to decision making.

Its logic, however, sometimes flies in the face of common sense. If £1 million has already been spent on a project which is now expected to return only £100,000, it may still be worthwhile spending £10,000 more if that is all that is required to complete the project. £1.01 million will have been spent to gain £100,000 but, right now, £1 million of the investment is irrecoverable. It is a sunk cost. It is irrelevant.

An illustration of the application of the sunk cost principle would be in appraising a programme which involves a pilot plant (or other feasibility study) being built before a main production facility. Before the pilot plant is built, its costs are a relevant part of the investment to be appraised. After it has been built and assessed, its costs are sunk, and only the experience is relevant for the continuing investment decision.

The economics of the sunk cost idea cannot be faulted. But it is important to learn from the experience of the sunk costs if they have been mismanaged, even if they cannot be recovered.

Opportunity costs

Opportunity cost is an economist's concept which recognizes that the choice of one alternative or option means forgoing the opportunity of taking the other alternative or one of the other options.

If you buy a second-hand car for £5,000 cash, and sell it after a year for £4,000, an accountant will tell you that the cost of owning the car was £1,000 (ignoring running costs). An economist will argue that using your £5,000 cash to buy the car meant that you gave up the opportunity of investing it and of earning interest of £500, say. For the economist, your cost of owning the car was £1,500 (depreciation of £1,000 plus an opportunity cost of £500). Opportunity cost can be an important concept in decision making, as the following example shows.

A company holds components which cost £10,000, and which are sufficient to make exactly 100 units of Product X. Their scrap value is £1,000 so that if they are scrapped the accountant will say that a loss of £9,000 has been incurred (£1,000 less £10,000). Assembling them will cost £2,000. Product X is obsolescent; there is a possibility of signing a final contract after which the chance of further sales is very limited. The contract price offered for the units is only £40 each. Should the contract be signed?

The cost accountant will say the contract will make a loss:

	£
Sales (100 units @ £40)	4,000
Less:	
components	(10,000)
assembly	(2,000)
	(12,000)
Loss	**£(8,000)**

The economist, however, will argue that the alternative to assembling the components is to scrap them. The opportunity cost of the

---

components for assembly is £1,000 – their value in the only feasible alternative.
For the economist:

	£
Sales (100 units @ £40)	4,000
Less:	
components	(1,000)
assembly	(2,000)
	(3,000)
Profit	**£1,000**

Break-even analysis

Cubrir gastos

Break-even analysis helps us to understand how total costs and profitability will alter with changes in the level of operations. It analyses the elements of operating profit by separating operating costs into fixed, variable and semi-variable elements before comparing them with sales revenue or turnover.

A cost is fixed if it does not change in response to short-term changes in the level of activity. For example, a managing director's salary will not vary with the volume of goods produced during any month; warehouse rates will not vary with small changes in a business's level of activity.

With time, of course, fixed costs will change, even for the same level of activity. Rentals will go up and salaries may increase. Fixed cost levels will change both because of management action and because of inflation. No cost will remain fixed for ever. Break-even analysis infers a time horizon, usually of a few weeks.

We must also recognize that fixed costs will not stay at the same level for any level of output. As output increases, they will change, but in 'step' increases (rather than gradually) to new levels. An expanding company may take on more supervisory and administrative staff, have to bear the depreciation cost of extra equipment and may invest in new buildings – see Figure 10.1 (a). These will all add 'step' increases to the level of fixed costs. Any analysis which shows a single level of fixed cost is only valid for fairly small changes in output level (the 'relevant range').

A variable cost is one that changes in response to changes in the level of activity. Raw materials are likely to be a major variable cost element for any manufacturing company. Total sales commissions and delivery expenses are other examples of costs which vary with the level of sales. Figure 10.1 (b) shows a variable cost curve for raw materials. Figure 10.1 (c) shows the trend in total costs.

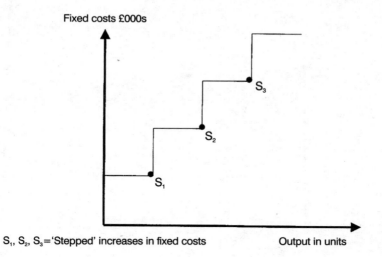

Fixed costs £000s

S_3

S_2

S_1

S_1, S_2, S_3 = 'Stepped' increases in fixed costs

Output in units

Figure 10.1 (a) *'Step' increases in fixed cost*

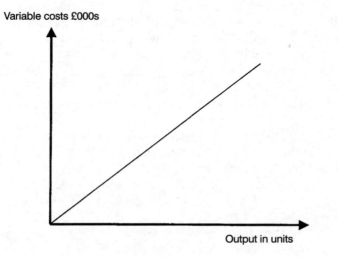

Variable costs £000s

Output in units

Figure 10.1 (b) *Material costs*

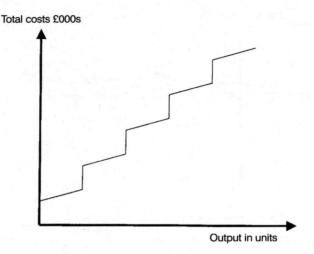

Figure 10.1 (c)   *Total costs*

When we draw a straight line for the variable cost curve, it infers that unit variable costs are constant, whatever the level of production. This is unlikely to be true. At low levels, inefficiencies are more likely. At the other extreme, when a plant is close to capacity, bottlenecks and delays may put unit costs up. However, between these limits, and for relatively small changes (of 10 per cent, say) around the current operating point, unit variable costs may be fairly constant.

In manufacturing, the cost of labour demonstrates the need to think carefully about how costs will behave with output changes. Direct labour is often cited as a variable cost. But whether it is or not depends heavily on the type of business. It is likely to be much easier to change the level of labour cost if demand drops in an assembly shop with many independent operatives. But in a process plant, the number and, therefore, the cost of plant operators may be fixed over quite large changes in output.

Finally, the definition of variable costs reinforces the need for a time horizon. Virtually no costs (apart from raw materials) will change in the next hour, even if production halts. To adjust direct labour by recruitment, wastage or laying-off needs time. Break-even analysis is based on a time horizon, which is based on the sort of decision being considered.

Semi-variable costs are of a hybrid nature, with fixed and variable elements. An example is telephone charges. The rental element is a fixed cost, whereas charges for calls made are a variable cost. In break-even analysis, these two components must be separated. The reason for separating costs into those that are variable and those that are fixed is that the result tells us how total costs will change if output falls or rises.

By plotting a company's fixed cost curve and then adding the variable cost curve for the expected levels of activity, the total cost curve shown in Figure 10.1 (d) is obtained. Alternatively, the same total cost curve can be drawn by starting with the variable cost line and then adding the fixed costs, as in Figure 10.1 (e).

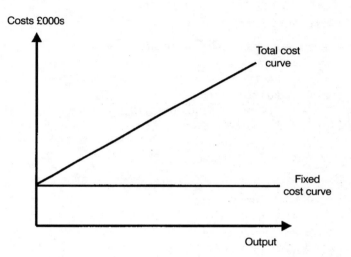

Figure 10.1 (d) *Total cost curve*

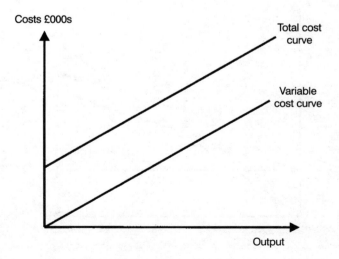

Figure 10.1 (e) *Total cost curves*

If a revenue curve is superimposed on the same graph as the cost curves, the result is the break-even chart; see Figure 10.1 (f). The revenue line shown is a straight line, inferring that prices remain unaltered as output varies.

Above the break-even point, revenues exceed total costs, and the diagram shows that a profit is made. Below the break-even point, total costs are not covered by revenue, and a loss results. At the break-even point, revenues match costs exactly.

The break-even point is where:

Revenue = fixed costs + variable costs.
If: p = unit price
         v = variable costs per unit
         F = fixed costs
         X = break-even volume in units
Then: $p.X = F + v.X$
and $X = F \div (p - v)$
The break-even sales revenue is $(p.X)$.

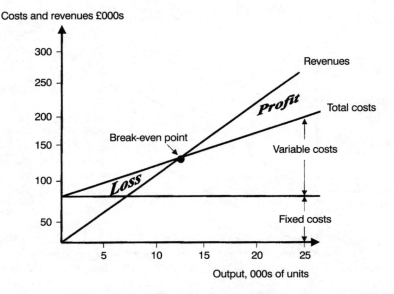

Figure 10.1 (f)   *Break-even diagram*

For example: **Kingsgate Limited** makes and sells only one product, which is priced at £10.00. The variable cost per unit is £5.00. Fixed costs total £75,000 per year. The maximum capacity is 25,000 units per year. Current utilization is 80 per cent of capacity.

The break-even sales volume is equal to:
Fixed costs (£75,000) ÷ (£10 less £5) = 15,000 units.
The break-even sales revenue is equal to:
£10 × 15,000 units = £150,000.
The sales volume required to meet an operating profit target of, say, £25,000 is equal to:
£25,000 + £75,000 ÷ (£10 less £5) = 20,000 units.
The sales revenue required to meet an operating profit target of, say, £25,000 is equal to:
20,000 units × £10 = £200,000.

A word of caution

You will have noticed that break-even analysis is built on a number of assumptions, particularly on the time-scale over which costs may vary, and the size of output changes. The straight lines of the diagrams probably hold good only for relatively limited changes about a company's current operating point. Beyond it, unit variable costs may change, as may prices or fixed cost levels.

The diagrams also assume that the levels of sales and output are equal, which may not be true in a manufacturing company. Finally, they do not cater easily for situations with a mix of products and/or services. However, break-even analysis is important for two reasons:

1. For the overall impression of the relative weightings of fixed and variable costs.
2. For a prediction of how profits will change over relatively small changes of output.

Contribution and marginal cost

The difference between revenue and variable costs is known as 'contribution':

Sales – variable costs = contribution

You can see this concept of contribution illustrated in Figure 10.1 (f). When output is very low, the difference between revenue and variable cost is very small. As output rises the revenue and variable cost grow

wider apart; contribution increases. At the break-even point, the contribution has grown so that it exactly equals the fixed costs. At break-even:

revenue = variable cost + fixed cost
revenue – variable cost = fixed cost
contribution = fixed cost.

As output increases above the break-even volume, the gap widens
further; the extra contribution produces profit. It is called 'contribution'
because it is the contribution that sales make to covering fixed costs and
earning a profit.

The contribution margin is the contribution expressed as a percentage
of revenues.

$$\text{Contribution margin} = \frac{(R - V)}{R} \times 100\%$$

where R = revenues and V = variable costs.

For example, Zurich Limited, year ended 31 December 1998:

Fixed costs	£80,000
Variable costs per unit	£120
Selling price per unit	£200

(1) Break-even point in units:
£80,000 divided by
unit contribution of £80 (£200 – £120) = 1,000 units
(2) Break-even point in terms of revenues or sales:
£80,000 divided by
contribution margin of 40%* = £200,000
*(£200 – £120) ÷ £200 × 100% = 40%.

The marginal cost of a product is the extra cost of producing one more
item. An extra product sold at above its marginal cost will produce
extra contribution which, if fixed costs are already covered, will
produce extra profit. This technique of pricing based on covering and
exceeding marginal costs is known as marginal cost pricing. The logic
of the approach is irrefutable. However, its undisciplined use can be
disastrous! Products or services priced at the margin do not recover
fixed costs. Marginal cost pricing may also damage the pricing
structure of existing products. This is not to say that marginal cost
pricing does not have a role if used cautiously. However, its occasional
use must not be allowed to hide the fact that products and services
should generate contribution rates adequate to cover fixed costs and
produce profits. Those with lower than average contribution rates must
be improved.

The importance of cost structure

The extent to which a company's profit changes as a result of a change in output directly reflects its cost structure. An understanding of this effect is crucial if a company has to make such real-life decisions as whether to match a drop in a competitor's price, or to accept the possible loss of sales that may result from an unaltered price.

Consider Figures 10.1 (g) and (h). Figure (g) shows a company with a high proportion of fixed costs, and Figure (h) shows a company with a high proportion of variable costs. Suppose both companies are operating at break-even. A small change in volume will have much more effect on the profits of the company in Figure (g) than it will on the other company. On the other hand, a small change in price (changing the slope of the revenue line) will shift the break-even point of the company in Figure (h) more than it will for the other company.

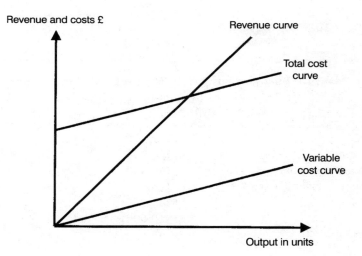

Figure 10.1 (g)   *Cost structure – relatively high fixed costs*

Conclusion

■ The profits of a company with relatively high fixed costs will be relatively more sensitive to changes in volume.
■ The profits of a company with relatively high variable costs will be relatively more sensitive to changes in margin (the difference between price and variable cost).

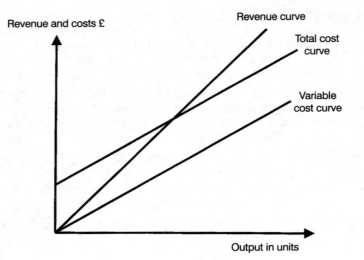

Figure 10.1 (h)   *Cost structure – relatively high variable costs*

The Beautiful Business Bureau (BBB) offers secretarial, telephone, telex and facsimile services to self-employed business people. In the last financial year, its results were:

	£
Sales	500,000
Variable costs	(40,000)
Semi-variable costs*	(40,000)
Fixed costs	(340,000)
	(420,000)
Trading profit	80,000

The **Corrugated Corkscrew Company** (CCC) manufactures accessories for home bars and cocktail cabinets. In the same period, its results were:

	£
Sales	500,000
Variable costs	(270,000)
Semi-variable costs*	(60,000)
Fixed costs	(90,000)
	(420,000)
Trading profit	80,000

*Assumes half of semi-variable costs are fully variable, and that half are fixed.

The managing directors of both companies coincidentally suggested an 8 per cent price increase. Both sales directors estimated that the result would be that customers providing 10 per cent of volume would take their business elsewhere.

- Does the price increase make sense? To BBB? To CCC?
- Which company is more volume sensitive?

Suggested answer:

BBB (£000s)

Sales (500 × 1.08 × 0.90)	486
Costs –	
variable (40 × 0.90)	(36)
semi-variable (20 × 0.90 + 20)	(38)
fixed	(340)
Operating profit (down 10%)	72

CCC (£000s)

Sales (500 × 1.08 × 0.90)	486
Costs –	
variable (270 × 0.90)	(243)
semi-variable (30 × 0.90 + 30)	(57)
fixed	(90)
Operating profit (up 20%)	96

You can see that, in the case of BBB, whose fixed costs are about 80 per cent of total costs, the effect of the 10 per cent reduction in volume is to reduce operating profit by 10 per cent. BBB is volume sensitive.

By contrast, CCC's cost structure is such that fixed costs make up only about 20 per cent of total costs. In this case, the effect of the 10 per cent volume reduction is to reduce the variable and semi-variable costs from £330,000 to £300,000 – a reduction of £30,000, or, as you would expect, 10 per cent. This saving in variable costs more than offsets the reduction in sales of £14,000 to give an overall increase in operating profit of £16,000. CCC is margin sensitive because its fortunes depend on the difference between sales and its variable costs, which are 80 per cent of total costs.

Key factor analysis

In any review of product profitability, it is important to maximize contribution for the factor that is in short supply. For example, the 1999 budget
for Southgate Limited is as follows:

	Product X	Product Y	Product Z	Total
Forecast sales volume (units)	10,000	5,000	6,000	
Expected revenues (£m)	1.50	0.95	1.56	4.01
Variable costs (£m)	(1.14)	(0.61)	(1.15)	(2.90)
Expected contribution (£m)	0.36	0.34	0.41	1.11
Contribution per unit	£36.00	£68.00	£68.33	

Each product has to go through three labour intensive processes: A, B
and C. The labour cost per hour is:

Process A: £3.00
Process B: £6.00
Process C: £3.00

The hours required for each product in each process are:

Product	Process hours
X	A = 12; B = 2.5; C = 6
Y	A = 10; B = 3; C = 3
Z	A = 15; B = 5; C = 12

The labour for process B is restricted in view of recruitment problems.
Southgate Limited should, therefore, seek to maximize contribution for
each hour of process B's labour:

Product	Contribution for each hour of Process B's labour
X	£36/2.5 hours = £14.40
Y	£68/3 hours = £22.67
Z	£68.33/5 hours = £13.67

This means that production should be ranked in the sequence product Y,
product X and then product Z up to the limit of the sales budget.

COSTING AND COSTING SYSTEMS

The second part of the chapter will build on the subjects covered in the
first. It will discuss a number of specific topics:

- What is the cost?
- Absorption and direct costing.
- Direct and allocated costs.

- Standard costing.
- Activity-based costing.
- Customer profitability analysis.

What is the cost?

Costing systems exist to answer the question 'What is the cost?' The question may be asked of a product, a service, a project; a staff-hour, an office; a department, a division; and so on. In the jargon, the product, unit or activity being costed is often referred to as the cost object. By contrast, a cost centre is an activity, function or location for which costs are collected, measured and reported, for example the finance function.

Costing systems have to recognize that there are some costs specific to the cost object, and that there are other costs common to a number of objects. These are often known as direct and indirect costs.

A *direct* cost is one that is directly attributable to the product or activity with which it is associated. It can be clearly identified as being incurred in the production of a product, or as part of the activity of a cost centre. In manufacturing, the cost of the raw materials used in the production of a product is a direct cost. Similarly, the cost of the employees who work on the products is usually considered a direct cost.

In an industry providing a standard service, such as banking, the cost object will usually be the individual service or transaction. The cost of the staff providing the service will be divided by the total number of transactions to arrive at the direct labour cost for each transaction. Where the service provided varies with the contract or job, the cost object often becomes a staff-hour. The total employment costs may be divided by contractual hours to give an hourly direct labour or staff cost.

An *indirect* cost is one that is incurred in support of an activity, but cannot be directly attributed to that activity. It is a cost necessary for the organization to function.

In manufacturing, support departments such as industrial engineering, production control and purchasing are normally classified as indirect. In a service organization handling large volumes of transactions, the information technology department may be considered to be an indirect cost.

Let us make two comments before continuing:

- At first sight, direct and indirect costs look very much like variable and fixed costs. The two sets of definitions are, in fact, very close. However, a fixed cost can be a direct cost (often called a direct overhead). For example, the depreciation of product tooling is a direct cost for that product.

- In practice, the precise definition of what is considered a direct cost and what is an indirect cost varies between organizations.

Absorption and direct costing

A costing system has little difficulty in identifying and attributing direct costs to the cost objects:

- direct materials and labour to a product;
- direct labour to a service (which might also have other small direct costs; stationery and postage, for example);
- direct employment costs to a staff-hour.

The term 'allocation of direct costs' is often used for this process, and a distinction is made between the allocation of direct costs and the apportionment and absorption of indirect costs. These terms are used later. However, 'allocation' is used in connection with apportioning indirect costs. It is in this last sense that it is most often met in business. It is when we come to the processing of indirect costs that the debate begins. There are two positions: full absorption costing and direct (or marginal) costing.

One approach is that the costs attributed to individual products or services should reflect all of the costs incurred in producing them. The indirect costs should be attributed in some way to the products, and the product costs should contain two elements:

1. The product's direct costs.
2. A recovery of a calculated proportion of indirect costs.

This process is known as 'full absorption costing', and is illustrated in Figure 10.2.

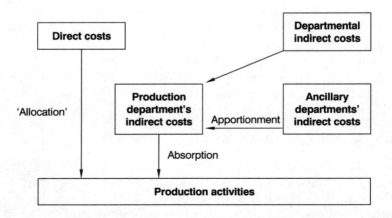

Figure 10.2   *Absorption costing*

Ancillary departments' indirect costs (for example, production control in a manufacturing company) must be apportioned between the various manufacturing departments (for example, the foundry, machine shop and assembly shop). Then, within each production department, the total of:

- its own indirect costs (for example, supervision and equipment depreciation);
- apportioned ancillary departments' indirect costs, which must be absorbed into the production costs of the products handled within the department.

The process requires:

- The development of rules for the apportionment of ancillary departments' indirect costs. The cost accountant sets out to apportion these costs in ways that reflect the economic structure of the firm. This can be a very controversial subject indeed. No matter how hard the accountant tries, he or she may fail to get agreement that the rules are either logical or fair. In fact, there may be little justification for some apportionments except that the costs have got to be passed on.
- Methods for transferring or absorbing indirect costs. Traditionally, this is done by applying an indirect 'overhead' rate to direct costs, often to direct labour costs alone. This is done at a rate normally derived from budgets; the budgeted indirect costs are divided by the budgeted direct costs to arrive at a budgeted overhead recovery rate.

An under- or over-recovery of overhead will result from a deviation from budget, for example:

- under- or over-production;
- a change of product mix;
- labour efficiencies or inefficiencies;
- indirect cost under- or over-spend.

Also, the rationale behind traditional absorption methods may have lost touch with reality. When labour costs were a large part of manufacturing costs, it may have made sense to allocate overheads as a loading on direct labour, but direct labour today is often only a fraction of total costs. A fresh look at absorption methods is, therefore, necessary if product costs are to reflect the 'true' economics.

Direct or marginal costing

In direct or marginal costing, only direct costs are attributed to products. Even direct overheads are excluded, so the direct costs included are really the variable or marginal costs. Indirect costs are not attributed to products; instead they become period costs (costs charged to the period s profit and loss account).

The system avoids the difficulty of apportionment and absorption. However, it requires all those working with the system to recognize that recovery of direct costs alone will not result in break-even (as it would under the full absorption system), and prices must be set with sufficient margin above direct costs to recover indirect costs as well.

Which is best?

Proponents of full absorption costing believe that it is important to know the full cost of a product or service. Otherwise, they argue, a price may be set below the level necessary to recover indirect costs and make an acceptable profit. Profit margins on old products may decline to the point where they no longer recover their fair share of indirect costs, and this must be made explicit by the cost system.

Supporters of direct costing argue that the allocations of full absorption costing are often arbitrary and, if uncorrected, may lead to wrong decisions. Secondly, since absorption rates are tied to budgeted volumes, the system is inflexible to variations in output. Product profitability can be sustained by ensuring contribution margin targets are high enough to recover indirect costs as well as to provide profit.

To deepen this discussion, let us look at an example which shows that the two systems may provide very different answers.

Suppose a company has three products, A, B and C, with equal sales. Its cost accountant, recognizing that the company's total budgeted indirect costs of £1,200,000 must be recovered, plans an overhead recovery rate of 200 per cent on the budgeted direct labour cost of £600,000.

The managing director, worried about the lack of profitability, asks for advice on which of the products to promote. The cost accountant provides the information below, based on budgeted figures:

Product	A	B	C	Total
Sales £000s	1,100	1,100	1,100	3,300
Direct labour hours 000s	17	33	50	100
Direct labour cost @ £6 per hour	(102)	(198)	(300)	(600)
Materials £000s	(700)	(500)	(300)	(1,500)
Indirect costs £000s	(204)	(396)	(600)	(1,200)

Cost of sales £000s	(1,006)	(1,094)	(1,200)	(3,300)
Gross profit £000s	94	6	**(100)**	0

The conclusion? In terms of profitability, A is better than B, which in turn is better than C, which shows a loss. Promote A, and either let C dwindle or cut it out!

A young assistant, with management accounting training, decides to try a direct costing approach, as shown below:

Product	A	B	C	Total
Sales £000s	1,100	1,100	1,100	3,300
Direct labour hours (000s)	17	33	50	100
Direct labour cost @ £6 per hour	(102)	(198)	(300)	(600)
Materials £000s	(700)	(500)	(300)	(1,500)
Cost of sales	(802)	(698)	(600)	(2,100)
Contribution	298	402	500	1,200
Indirect costs				(1,200)
Gross profit				0

To the assistant, C is the best product. Her advice would be to promote C, and let A starve for resources.

Who is right? It depends on the extent to which the indirect costs can genuinely be attributed to any of the products. If they cannot, then the assistant's analysis of contribution is the more meaningful. It shows that all products are making positive contributions to overheads, and the company cannot drop any of them. Indeed, if product C is cut, the company will be worse off (through a loss of contribution) by £500,000, rather than benefiting by £100,000 through avoiding the loss shown by the first approach. If the indirect costs are genuinely unattributable, and would not be reduced if C were to be dropped, the loss of contribution would be reflected by an equivalent overall loss.

The difference in the product rankings provided by the two systems clearly arises from the association of indirect costs with direct labour costs and the very different proportions of labour and material in the individual product cost structures. If the indirect cost loadings were made on direct material, for example, the product rankings would be reversed. (Try it!)

The example shows clearly that *product-line analysis* is more meaningful if direct costing is used. A word of warning is, however, appropriate. Direct costing tends to recognize only variable costs as direct costs. We noted earlier that there can be direct fixed costs. Product-line analysis must recognize such direct overheads. For example, if the indirect costs include the depreciation of machinery used only in the production of Product C, that direct overhead should be deducted before C's contribution is compared with other products.

Many management accountants feel that direct costing is more helpful and it is in use in some companies for management accounts. However, a consequence of the system is that stocks are valued at direct cost without any element of the overheads incurred in producing them. Professional accountants feel this is inappropriate, and accounting convention requires that published accounts have stock valuations which include production overheads. Similarly, direct costing systems are not acceptable to the tax authorities. For these reasons, and because of a persistent belief among many managers that it is vital to know the 'full' cost of a product, service or department, full absorption systems continue to flourish, despite the attractions of direct costing.

Standard costing

Standard costing is a technique that sets predetermined estimates of the cost of manufacturing goods and providing services. These predetermined estimates are then compared to the actual costs that have been incurred. The differences between the predetermined standards and the actual costs are analysed into variances. This technique is referred to as variance analysis.

Standard costing has five basic elements:

1. Setting resource and efficiency levels using approaches such as process improvement (total quality management), labour and material specifications as well as labour and material price projections.
2. Calculating the standard cost for labour, material and indirect costs for each product and service. The standards should not represent the ideal situation since they may be unattainable and, therefore, demotivating. However, they should be stretching to stimulate improvements in efficiency.
3. Setting standard selling prices for each product.
4. Working out the variances (whether favourable or unfavourable) between the actual cost and the standard cost.
5. Understanding the 'root' causes of the variances. There are two main types of variances – those relating to price and those relating to volume as explained in the example below.

St Michael's Limited

	£m
Budgeted operating profit for November 1998	7.0
Actual operating profit for November 1998	7.4
Variance	0.4F
Selling price variance	0.9F
Sales volume variance	0.7U
Material price variance	0.5F
Material usage variance	0.3U
Labour rate variance	0.2U
Labour efficiency variance	0.1F
Overhead expenditure variance	0.5F
Overhead volume variance	0.4U
Total	**0.4F**

(F = favourable; U = unfavourable)

An explanation of the variances can then be given.

The operating profit for November is £400,000 higher than anticipated because:

- Higher selling prices were obtained (£0.9mF).
- Cheaper material buying-in prices were negotiated (£0.5mF).
- The labour aspects of production were completed faster than expected (£0.1mF).
- Indirect costs (overheads) were lower than expected (£0.5mF).
- Sales volumes were lower than expected (£0.7mU).
- Additional amounts of bought-in material were used (£0.3mU).
- Labour costs were higher than predicted (£0.2mU).
- Indirect costs were not recovered sufficiently in view of the lower sales volume (£0.4mU).

Once the initial explanations have been highlighted, the next task is to investigate why the variances occurred. For example:

- Labour costs were higher than anticipated because skill shortages forced up the rates of pay.
- Material costs were lower than expected because the strength of sterling reduced the sterling costs of imported raw materials.

Activity-based costing

In early factories, direct labour was often the highest production expense (apart, possibly, from the cost of materials). It seemed to make sense to associate the relatively low overheads with the activity of the shop floor and, in the costing systems, recover them through a loading on direct labour rates.

In today's modern factories, the impact of technology has meant that the proportion of a product's total cost contributed by direct labour has shrunk dramatically, often to 15 per cent or less. Recognition that the machine time used in making a product was a more valuable resource than the direct labour required meant that some companies switched to recovering part or all of their overheads on machine hours rather than on direct labour hours. It is not uncommon for companies to recover some overheads – such as depreciation, power and maintenance – on machine hours, and others – such as supervision – on direct labour. Another common variation is to recover materials management costs – such as procurement, inspection, storage and handling – as a loading on the value of direct materials. Here is an example.

Suppose that we have a factory with three products, X, Y and Z. All three are similar and, while they require different raw materials, need much the same material cost and machine and assembly time. A conventional costing system, charging overheads based on the volume of direct labour, direct material or machine time required for each product, will end up with very similar unit costs for each of X, Y and Z.

However, Product X has a steady demand, is responsible for the bulk of the factory's output, and is made in large batches. Scheduling is simple; purchasing is orderly; large product volumes result from each machine set-up. Products Y and Z suffer from sporadic and uneven demand and are, therefore, made in frequent but irregular and much smaller batches than Z. Scheduling is more complex; purchase orders are much smaller and relatively more frequent, and need chasing to achieve a balanced supply for production; relative stock levels of materials and finished products are higher, reflecting the variability of demand, and only short production runs are possible before machines are reset.

In this situation, it will be obvious that the balance of the efforts of overhead departments such as production scheduling, purchasing and materials handling and of the incidence of overhead costs, such as machine set-ups, will be tilted towards Y and Z. Note that the size and, therefore, the costs, of support departments are very largely fixed in the short term. They are set at a level appropriate for handling all three products, and are influenced by the relative complexity of managing Y and Z. It seems reasonable that Y and Z should carry a higher proportion of the overheads. Nevertheless, under a conventional costing system, the bulk of the overheads will be carried by X; Product X effectively subsidizes Y and Z.

If Product X is in a highly competitive market, the cost of subsidizing overheads generated by Y and Z may make its profitability suspect. On the other hand, the subsidized costs of Y and Z may make them appear more attractive than they really are. Incorrect judgements of product line attractiveness and profitability may result.

Activity-based costing (ABC) tries to match the cost of support functions to the demand caused by products for that support. It reasons that activities, rather than volumes, cause support overheads. It seeks to ensure that, if the production of a product causes activities, the costs of those activities are reflected in the product cost.

ABC first attempts to identify the business reasons (the cost drivers) which generate overheads. As in a conventional system, it will recognize that some variable overheads such as electricity can be directly associated with volume.

ABC then identifies the main causes of overheads. What are the reasons for the size and the fixed overhead costs of the purchasing department or of production control? What are the transactions that their staff carry out, and how do these transactions affect the department's size and cost? The main transactions determining the size of the purchasing department or production control might be the number of purchase orders placed or the number of production batches scheduled. These are the cost drivers that affect purchasing and production control costs.

A support department's activities may be caused by more than one cost driver. For example, if much of the purchasing department's time is spent approving supplier invoices, the costs of the department might be apportioned between two drivers: the number of orders and the number of invoices.

It should also be recognized that increasing the number of cost drivers increases the system's complexity, and it will only be worthwhile if product costs are materially affected. For example, if there is little significant variation in the number of supplier invoices generated by each order, little improvement in costs will result from adding the second driver of supplier invoices. It will only be worthwhile if a small number of orders generate a disproportionate number of supplier invoices, and if these orders result from the production of some, but not all, of the products.

Cost centres, or cost 'pools', are set up for each cost driver. One cost driver may affect a number of support departments. For example, the number of purchase orders placed will affect receiving, inspection and, perhaps, materials handling as well as purchasing. Departments apportion their overall costs to the cost pools of the cost drivers that affect them, according to a judgement of the extent to which each of the drivers causes their costs. This process is illustrated in Figure 10.3.

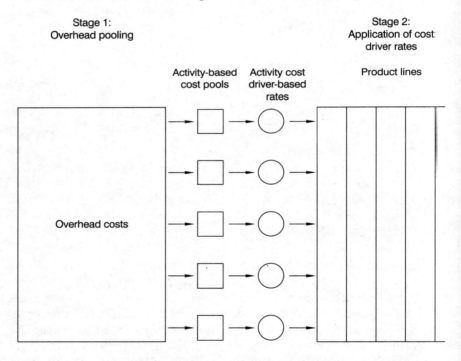

Figure 10.3   *Activity-based costing*

The total costs apportioned to the cost driver pools are used to derive the activity cost rate. For example, if the total cost for a period in the purchase order driver pool is £750,000, and the number of purchase orders forecast to be issued during the period is 5,000, then the activity cost charge rate is £150 per purchase order.

Once the charge rates are established for each pool, they can be applied to the products. This requires an estimate, by product, of the level of activity it will generate for each driver. If the forecast production of 10,000 units of Product P, for example, is expected to generate 50 purchase orders, Product P will be charged with £7,500 (50 times £150), and the unit cost will increase by 75p.

ABC has been developed largely in response to concerns about the effectiveness of traditional product costing systems used to determine product manufacturing costs. In a traditional system, the difference between the revenue generated by a product and its total manufacturing costs is the product's gross profit for the period, and the gross profit divided by the sales revenue yields the product's gross margin. Gross margins are often compared in product-line analysis.

If the company is to show an operating profit, the total gross profit made by all products must exceed the company's sales, marketing, distribution and administration costs. In management accounts, such costs are treated as period costs, charged off against the gross profit for the period. However, it will be evident that some products may generate more sales and marketing costs than others – and, therefore, need to show higher gross margins in order to be equally profitable. Similarly, warehouse capacity will be adjusted to suit the needs of all of the company's products, but may be used more extensively by some products than others.

ABC provides a tool to analyse and apportion to products, overheads which are traditionally charged off to the period. In identifying the activities that generate the overheads, and linking the activities to the products they support, understanding of 'true' product profitability can only be improved.

Customer profitability analysis

Traditionally, the attention of management accountants and their accounting systems has tended to focus on the profitability of products and services rather than customers. However, this is beginning to change as it is realized that factors such as selling prices, distribution costs, discounts and payment terms all have a major impact on overall profitability. Accordingly, a profit and loss account can be prepared to assess the relative profitability of customers as well as the relative profitability of products. It is applying the principles of activity-based costing to customers rather than just to products. An example is given below.

North Walls Ltd

Customer Profitability Statement for the three months ended 31 December 1998 (£000s)

Sales (at list prices)	200
Discounts	(12)
Net sales	188
Cost of sales	(98)
Gross profit	90
Distribution costs	(20)
Selling costs	(10)
Cost of working capital	(5)
Customer contribution	**55**

Notes:

1. *Sales (at list prices)*. This should be the benchmark since it establishes a common baseline for differences between customers.
2. *Discounts*. These are a reflection of the relative power of individual customers and include such items as quantity discounts and special offers at different times of the year like Easter and Christmas.
3. *Cost of sales*. This reflects the direct costs of the goods and services sold to customers and will reflect the mix of the goods and services provided. For each customer, it is important to identify the proportion of relatively high (and relatively low) margin products and services sold and to assess what can be done to improve the mix and to increase the gross profit and the gross profit percentage (the gross margin).
4. *Distribution costs*. The distance and the frequency of deliveries should be taken into account as well as the extent to which special warehousing facilities need to be provided.
5. *Selling costs*. These should reflect the time and expenses involved in maintaining the accounts of different customers, such as the frequency of sales representatives' calls and the involvement of more senior sales and marketing staff such as sales managers and the marketing director.
6. *Working capital*. There are two important aspects. First, the extent to which there are specific requirements for holding stock. Second, the cost of granting credit. Customers who pay their bills faster are less expensive than those who are slow.

SUMMARY

Costs

To make a correct economic decision it is essential to focus on differential or incremental costs. These are the costs that change as a result of taking one decision rather than another. The word 'cost' by itself is not very helpful. We need to know if the costs under discussion are fixed, variable, total, direct, indirect, or marginal, just to give some examples.

Break-even analysis supports an understanding of how total costs and profitability will change as output changes. In particular, it is important to understand a company's cost structure and, especially, the relative proportions of fixed and variable costs.

The difference between sales and variable costs is called 'contribution'. It has a crucial role to play in marginal costing and product profitability analysis as well as in marginal cost pricing. These techniques need to be used with care.

Key factor analysis focuses attention on the resource that is in short supply.

Costing and costing systems

Costing systems are designed to answer the question 'What did the product or service cost?' Caution needs to be exercised in calculating 'total' cost because it may contain an element of indirect cost that has been calculated somewhat arbitrarily. Caution is also required in working out direct costs since they do not provide the complete cost picture. These issues are particularly relevant in an assessment of relative product profitability.

Standard costing is a technique to compare predetermined cost estimates with the actual costs that have been incurred. The differences or variances can then be investigated and corrective action taken.

Activity-based costing is a relatively new technique, which is designed to overcome some of the problems of full absorption costing. It stresses that activities, not output, cause costs and it seeks to ensure that these activities are reflected in the product cost.

Customer profitability analysis seeks to apply the principles of activity-based costing to customers rather than just to products.

CHAPTER 11

Budgetary Control

INTRODUCTION

The purpose of this chapter is to introduce the major aspects of financial planning and control. Planning and control are two vitally important tasks in ensuring that the finances of a business are managed effectively. Short-term plans are referred to as budgets. They have a 12-month time-scale and focus on profitability and cash flow.

A budget is stated in quantitative terms. It represents the desired financial picture for the next 12 months. In practice, it is a 'contract' since managers give a commitment that a certain set of targets will be achieved. BP, for example, uses the term 'Performance Contract' rather than budget. The budget is normally firm for its life so that the 'budget is the budget' even if economic circumstances change during the budget period. The period itself is broken down into shorter control periods of a calendar month or a quarter, so that the budget can be phased to allow, for example, for seasonal fluctuations.

BUDGETARY CONTROL

'Budgetary control' means that for each activity or collection of activities, actual performance is monitored against the budget. This enables differences or variances to be highlighted. They can then be investigated and corrective action can be taken to help to ensure that the actual results and the budgeted results become as close as possible. This is explained in Figure 11.1.

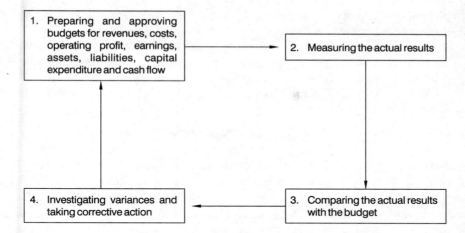

Figure 11.1 *The budgetary control cycle*

An effective system of budgetary control enables the 'top' management team to:

- decentralize and to delegate responsibility;
- co-ordinate all financial activities so as to achieve agreed objectives within clear constraints and guidelines;
- retain overall control;
- monitor managers' performance;
- prepare regular forecasts which are (or should be) independent, objective estimates of what the results for the budget period are likely to be in the light of actual performance so far. These forecasts or latest estimates are quite separate from the budget. However, they do enable management teams to prepare for the consequences of new developments such as competitor activity and market growth.

The process of budgeting and budgetary control applies to the business as a whole. It starts several months before the beginning of the next financial year when the head office or parent company issues guidelines to each activity – which may be large subsidiary companies with their own portfolio of activities. These guidelines will cover all the principal financial aspects including expectations about the growth in operating profit, earnings and the levels of capital expenditure which are compatible with cash flow projections and an acceptable debt to equity ratio.

Experience suggests that these guidelines are sometimes ignored or only partially taken into account by individual operating companies so that the first 'round' of budget submissions received by the parent company may not be consistent with its overall requirements. A robust and protracted exchange of views between the centre and subsidiary companies then takes place and new budget submissions will have to be prepared to ensure that they meet the criteria laid down by head office!

As a result of this process, the 'top' management team will be more confident that changes in its business environment have been carefully considered, that different options for achieving its budget objectives have been identified and that resources have been allocated efficiently.

PREPARING THE BUDGET

The preparation of the sales budget is the starting point for the preparation of the overall or master budget. The marketing and sales team will need to consider the present level of trading, anticipate future conditions, and use feedback from the sales force and market research to prepare a sales budget. The sales budget, of course, is not a single figure for the financial year but a detailed analysis of sales based on selling prices and sales volumes as follows:

- by product and service offering;
- by customer;
- by region;
- by month.

Once the first draft of the sales budget has been completed, the production or operations budget can be put together. In the case of a manufacturing company, the sales budget will need to be considered and allowances will need to be made for changes in stock levels, the use of sub-contractors and lead times so that the full operational implications of the sales budget can be highlighted. These will focus on:

- the level of output by product and service line;
- when it is needed;
- which activities or departments will produce it; and
- the associated costs of the labour, materials and facilities.

The sales and operations budgets determine the level of activity for the whole of the organization. This affects the resources required for marketing, the sales force, distribution, and administrative activities such as finance and human resources which will need to prepare their own cost budgets.

The budget-setting process is illustrated in Figure 11.2. In the case of a non-manufacturing or service business such as an advertising agency or a management consultancy, there will be no 'cost of goods sold' or 'production' budget. Instead, the focus of attention will be the 'operating cost' budget which will be particularly concerned with (a) personnel costs, and (b) the cost of facilities such as office accommodation and information technology.

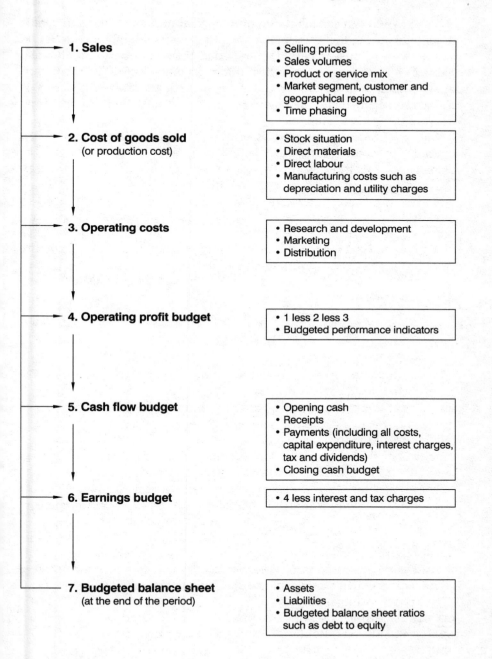

1. Sales
- Selling prices
- Sales volumes
- Product or service mix
- Market segment, customer and geographical region
- Time phasing

2. Cost of goods sold
(or production cost)
- Stock situation
- Direct materials
- Direct labour
- Manufacturing costs such as depreciation and utility charges

3. Operating costs
- Research and development
- Marketing
- Distribution

4. Operating profit budget
- 1 less 2 less 3
- Budgeted performance indicators

5. Cash flow budget
- Opening cash
- Receipts
- Payments (including all costs, capital expenditure, interest charges, tax and dividends)
- Closing cash budget

6. Earnings budget
- 4 less interest and tax charges

7. Budgeted balance sheet
(at the end of the period)
- Assets
- Liabilities
- Budgeted balance sheet ratios such as debt to equity

Figure 11.2   *The budget-setting process*

There are additional important points to bear in mind when a budget is being prepared. First, do make sure that you understand the actual results for the current period – the period before the start of the budget period – so that the impact of the different factors affecting overall performance, such as the product mix and the breakdown of operating costs, is fully appreciated. This will help to ensure that next year's budget fully reflects these inter-relationships.

Second, be clear about what is going to be different in the next budget period. For example, the introduction of a new product range and the expansion of facilities will affect the overall revenue and cost structure. These differences need to be reflected in the budget.

Third, take care to specify all the assumptions you have used in preparing the various drafts of the budget. Sales volumes, selling prices, head count, and percentage salary increases are all examples. Your budget submissions will almost certainly be challenged and if you are not clear about the assumptions on which they were based, it will be very difficult to defend them since there will be no benchmarks against which they can be justified.

FLEXIBLE BUDGETING

Flexible budgeting involves the preparation of not just one, but a series of budgets for varying levels of activity. The aim is to allow the comparison of the actual costs incurred with a flexed budget which corresponds to the level of activity actually achieved. A fixed budget, by contrast, is a budget prepared for a level of activity determined at the outset and left unchanged thereafter. The consequence of this is that any variance resulting from a comparison of an actual cost with a budgeted cost can be misleading, since the actual cost is being compared with a budgeted cost for a level of activity which did not materialize. This can be overcome by the use of a flexible budgeting system. For example:

Expenditure Report

(A) Fixed budget at 100% level of activity (B) Variance (C) Actual cost (D) Variance (E) Flexible budget at actual level of activity (80%)

(A)	(B)	(C)	(D)	(E)
£2m→	£0.25m (F)→	£1.75m→	£0.15m (U)→	£1.60m

A misleading favourable (F) variance of £0.25m is reported on a fixed budgeting system. The flexible budgeting system reports, correctly, an unfavourable (U) variance of £0.15m.

ZERO-BASED BUDGETING (ZBB)

The ZBB approach starts with a 'clean sheet' and seeks to question the entire budget. It endeavours to prepare budgets from scratch. In this way, managers are forced to justify their resource requirements, which are expressed as costs in their budgets. Each item of expenditure is challenged. The first step is to question whether the expenditure should exist at all and it is only then that budgeted expenditure levels are arrived at. The essence of ZBB is to explore better ways of working which would result in lower costs, and it is a philosophy that may be applied throughout an organization.

ZBB is very consistent with Business Process Re-engineering (BPR). The proponents of BPR argue that a company should organize itself around 'customer-driven' core processes such as order fulfilment and new product development. They contend that the traditional approach to budgeting is incrementalist – it is only concerned with a short-term time horizon and with minor changes and improvements, which tends to perpetuate serious inefficiencies. BPR, by contrast, advocates a fundamental challenging of the status quo.

In terms of resource allocation, for example, SmithKline Beecham operates a system which forces managers to generate at least four different options to achieve a given objective and each option is subject to an independent financial review. The options are:

1. The current plan (existing proposals).
2. 'Buy up' (provide additional expenditure).
3. 'Buy down' (provide less expenditure).
4. 'The minimal plan' which involves abandoning a project but using the lessons of the experience for other opportunities.

BUDGET MANAGEMENT

The comparison of actual results with the budget can take place at two levels. First, at an activity or departmental level, when a manager is provided, for example, with information about costs. The actual costs are compared with the budgeted costs for the month under review with a further comparison for the cumulative number of months in the financial year. An example is shown in Figure 11.3.

In the report, a distinction has been drawn between controllable and non-controllable expenditure. This allows the manager concerned to monitor progress against the budget for which he or she has both responsibility and authority (controllable costs). Non-controllable costs such as

Department... Month..							
Cost code	Description	Current month			Year to date		
		Actual (a) £m	Budget (b) £m	(a) as a % of (b)	Actual (a) £m	Budget (b) £m	(a) as a % of (b)
320	Controllable: – Personnel costs	3.4	3.6	94.4%	24.3	23.0	105.7%
710	Non-controllable: – Head office charges	1.1	1.0	110.0%	7.7	7.0	110.0%

Figure 11.3   *Managing the budget: comparing actual and budgeted costs*

head office charges are reported separately so that the fuller picture of responsibility without authority can be given.

The second level of the comparison of actual costs with budgeted costs takes place at the top of the organization – board level. From this viewpoint, a global approach is used so that the corporate budgeted figures for example, profit and loss accounts, cash flow statements and balance sheets are compared with the actual results for each month and year to date.

The variances disclosed in the monthly budget report will need to be investigated, but although that is necessary, it is not sufficient. Corrective action is required too. An indication is also needed as to how long it will take before the corrective action becomes effective. For example, an overspend in one month is not necessarily critical if the year to date position is satisfactory. In the case of the monthly budget report, the current month's personnel costs are 5.6 per cent (or £200,000 below budget). However, the year to date position is unsatisfactory since personnel costs are 5.7 per cent or £1.3 million above budget. This may be due to excessive overtime payments, which may have to be reduced.

SUMMARY

In the short term, the budget is *the* crucial financial control mechanism. It enables actual results to be compared with budgeted performance. As a consequence, differences or variances can be highlighted and corrective action can be taken. The budget-setting process is a seven-stage exercise starting with the sales budget and then moving on to the cost budget so that a budgeted profit and loss account can be prepared. Finally, a cash flow projection is necessary so that a budgeted balance sheet can be compiled.

It is most important to be clear about the assumptions on which a budget is based so that it can be defended in 'challenge' sessions.

Apart from traditional budgeting, other budgeting techniques include flexible budgeting and zero-based budgeting.

CHAPTER 12

Investment Appraisal

INTRODUCTION

Capital investment decisions are crucially important ones because they are the way in which an organization implements its corporate strategy. For this reason, the economic case for a project should be much more than a purely financial appraisal. There are likely to be strategic, marketing and human resource implications, which cannot be considered with a purely financial orientation. The appraisal of investment projects is not just a set of financial calculations but an overall business review to consider how competitive advantage will be sustained. The scope of the decisions involved is extremely wide and includes:

- *Expansion* – additions to existing facilities such as production capacity and warehousing. A good example is the proposed new Terminal 5 at Heathrow Airport.
- *Cost reduction* – deciding whether to replace old assets with new ones in order to achieve operating efficiencies, for example, the upgrading of rolling stock by the privatized train operating companies.
- *Market development* – assessing the viability of an investment such as the development, marketing and launch of a new product or service, for example, Virgin's entry into financial services.
- *Acquisitions and disposals* – appraising the acquisition of other businesses and the disposal of businesses and assets to external parties, for example, the acquisition of Amoco by British Petroleum.
- *Lease or buy* – determining whether to purchase an asset outright or to finance it under a lease agreement.

The objective of an investment appraisal is to assess the viability of the opportunities by comparing the expected benefits with the anticipated costs.

The purpose of this chapter is to explain the various methods and to describe some of the practical issues that need to be considered.

PROJECT APPRAISAL TECHNIQUES

The return on investment

The criterion for accepting an investment proposal will be a minimum rate of return which must be achieved, for example, over the expected life of the project. This is explained below and in the comments that follow.

Accounting rate of return

Year		Project A £000s	Project B £000s	Project C £000s
0	Investment	(200)	(300)	(300)
1	Profit	15	5	55
2	Profit	15	15	45
3	Profit	15	25	35
4	Profit	15	35	25
5	Profit	15	45	15
6	Profit	15	55	5
Total profit		**90**	**180**	**180**

Note that:

1. The convention is to say that Year 0 is today or 'now'. Year 1 is 12 months from now. Year 2 is 24 months away. Year 3 is 36 months away and so on.
2. For the sake of simplicity, the benefits and costs associated with the investment proposal are assumed to occur at the end of the relevant year.
3. For projects A, B and C there are initial investments of £200,000 and £300,000 which produce expected profits of £90,000, £180,000 and £180,000 respectively. 'Profit' for this purpose is defined as profit *after* taxation but *before* interest or financing charges. Tax is a cost like any other cost and should, therefore, be allowed for in the calculations. Financing costs should be excluded because it is the trading benefits of the project that are being assessed. How the project is financed is a quite separate matter.

The average annual profit for each of the projects is as follows:
   A (£90,000 ÷ 6 years) = £15,000
   B (£180,000 ÷ 6 years) = £30,000
   C (£180,000 ÷ 6 years) = £30,000
The average rate of return for each of the projects is as follows:
   A (£15,000 ÷ the opening investment of £200,000 x 100%) = 7.5%
   B (£30,000 ÷ the opening investment of £300,000 x 100%) = 10%
   C (£30,000 ÷ the opening investment of £300,000 x 100%) = 10%

Based on the calculations, the conclusions from using the rate of return method are:

- The rates of return on the three projects suggest that project A is inferior to projects B and C. However, the rate of return is identical for projects B and C.
- The rate of return makes no allowance for the fact that immediate profits, as in the case of C, are more valuable than distant ones as in the case of B. Thus, the rate of return does not consider the *time value of money* and it is based on *accounting* profit rather than cash flow.
- The rate of return is an arbitrary yardstick. The opportunity cost of capital is ignored. This is the best rate of return that could be earned from comparable investment opportunities elsewhere.

The payback method

In this case, companies specify that the initial outlay – the opening investment – should be recovered within a specified time period. The payback period is calculated by counting the number of years it takes for the cumulative benefits to equal the initial outlay. An example is given below.

Payback Period

Year		Project A £000s	Project B £000s	Project C £000s
0	Investment	(120)	(160)	(180)
1	Profit	30	80	30
2	Profit	30	80	60
3	Profit	30	40	90
4	Profit	30	20	100
5	Profit	30	10	120
Payback period		**4 Years**	**2 Years**	**3 Years**

The conclusions regarding the use of the payback method are:

■ Project B, with the shortest payback, is the most attractive option.
■ The benefits after the payback period are ignored. In the case of project C, for example, the estimated profits in years 4 and 5 are not taken into account at all. No weight is given to the more distant benefits. By contrast, the rate of return method gives these benefits too much weight.
■ A payback period has to be decided upon. If the same payback period is used regardless of the project life, too many short-life projects and too few long-life projects will be accepted.
■ The payback period is not a measure of profitability. It is more of an indicator of risk since it focuses on the 'exposure period' before the initial cost of an investment is recovered.

Cash flow, present value and net present value

You will recall that the rate of return depends on accounting profit. Accounting profit is recognized when it is earned rather than when cash is received from customers and cash payments are made to suppliers. We have also indicated that an assessment of an investment should be determined not only by the level of the benefits, but when they materialize. Therefore, an estimate is required of the cash flows, both positive and negative, which are attributable directly to the project, and their timing.

Under the conventions of accounting, cash outflows are split into two categories – current or revenue expenditure such as advertising and salaries, and capital expenditure. Current expenditure is deducted from revenues when calculating profit, but capital expenditure is not since it is written off over a number of years by way of a depreciation charge that is deducted from profit. As a consequence, profits include some cash flows and exclude others and they are reduced by depreciation charges which are not cash flows at all. Depreciation should, therefore, be excluded from the cash flow calculations.

A rich aunt, Noreen, proposes to give you a gift of £50,000. She wonders whether you would prefer the £50,000 now or in a year's time. This is not a difficult decision! You would prefer the £50,000 now because the £50,000 today is worth more than in 12 months' time because it can be invested immediately to earn a rate of return. Therefore, the present value of £50,000, if it was receivable in a year, can be calculated by multiplying the £50,000 by a discount factor which is less than one. .

For example, assume that an annual return of 5 per cent is available on an investment of £50,000. You would be indifferent about receiving the £50,000 in a year or receiving £50,000 x 1/1.05 = £47,620 now. £47,620 invested now at 5 per cent will grow to £50,000 at the end of 12 months.

The 1/1.05 (which equals 0.95) is the discount factor and £47,620 is the present value of the £50,000 receivable in a year at a return of 5 per cent.

Obviously, present values will change as the rates of return change and the timing of the cash flows alter. For instance, the present value of £50,000 receivable in two years' time at a return of 5 per cent will be £50,000 x 1/(1.05) x 1/(1.05) = £45,500.

The new discount factor is 0.91 (1/(1.05)²). Discount factors for different rates of return and for different time periods are given in Appendix C.

The rate of return used in an investment appraisal is referred to as the 'discount rate', the 'hurdle rate' or the 'opportunity cost of capital'. It is called the opportunity cost because it is the return foregone by investing in one particular project rather than another. The cost of capital will be discussed in more detail later.

Your aunt has changed her mind. She now insists on giving you £50,000 in 12 months' time. At a return of 5 per cent, this is equivalent, as we have seen, to a present value of £47,620. Your aunt is also becoming more eccentric. She tells you that she will not give you the £50,000 at all unless you buy a holiday cottage in Scotland without delay. This is expected to cost £25,000. The net present value of Aunt Noreen's project is, therefore, the present value of £47,620 less the outlay on the cottage, to give £22,620. By agreeing to Noreen's stipulation, you will be £22,620 better off.

This idea of net present value (NPV for short) can now be extended tc assess the viability of a more conventional investment opportunity.

Kingsgate Limited is considering a small investment. It estimates the pattern of cash inflows and outflows as follows:

Year	Cash inflow/(outflow) £000s
0	(10)
1	3
2	3
3	3
4	3
5	3

The opportunity cost of capital is 10 per cent. What is the project's NPV?

Year	Cash inflow/ (outflow) £000s	Discount factor at 10%	Present value of cash inflow/(outflow) £000s
0	(10)	1	(10)
1	3	0.91	2.73
2	3	0.83	2.49
3	3	0.75	2.25
4	3	0.68	2.04
5	3	0.62	1.86
NPV			**1.37**

Kingsgate will be £1,370 better off by investing in the project than by not doing so. The word 'net' in net present value means the sum of the positive and negative present values of the cash flows during the life of the project.

The advantages of the NPV approach are:

- It recognizes that receiving £1 today is worth more than receiving £1 later. This is because the £1 today can be invested to earn a return immediately.
- It focuses on the estimated cash flows from the project and the opportunity cost of capital.
- Present values are today's values. Therefore, the present values of all the cash inflows and outflows can be added up to calculate a net present value for the project as a whole.

Internal rate of return

You can see from the Kingsgate example above that as the discount rate increases, the discount factor for a given year will fall. For example, if the discount rate was 20 per cent, the discount factor for year 3 would be $1/(1.20)^3$. This is equal to 0.58 rather than the 0.75 at a discount rate of 10 per cent. Eventually, as the discount rate continues to be increased, the point will be reached when the NPV of the cash flows will be precisely equal to zero. The discount rate at which this happens is called the 'internal rate of return' (IRR) or the 'discounted cash flow' (DCF) rate of return.

For Kingsgate, the NPV of the cash flows will be zero at a discount rate of about 15 per cent. (In practice, it is calculated by the use of a spreadsheet model.) At 10 per cent, however, the project has an NPV of £1,370. The company could borrow £10,000 and, with the cash flows in years 1–5 repay the capital outlay of £10,000 and generate a surplus of £1,370. This is comparable to a repayment mortgage.

Year	Opening balance £000s	Interest at 10%	Total amount £000s	Cash flow £000s	Closing balance £000s
1	11.37*	1.14	12.51	3.0	9.51
2	9.51	0.95	10.46	3.0	7.46
3	7.46	0.75	8.21	3.0	5.21
4	5.21	0.52	5.73	3.0	2.73
5	2.73	0.27	3.00	3.0	–

*The initial outlay of £10,000 plus the NPV of £1,370.

The rule in investment appraisal is that a project should be accepted on economic criteria if the IRR is greater than the opportunity cost of capital.

Kingsgate's IRR works out at 15 per cent. The cost of capital is 10 per cent. Therefore, the IRR exceeds the cost of capital and the project should be accepted. Another way of coming to the same conclusion is to accept a project if the NPV is positive at the cost of capital. At 10 per cent (the cost of capital), the NPV is £1.37 million.

If the IRR is less than the cost of capital, the project should be rejected. This is the same as saying that the NPV of the project is negative at the cost of capital.

The IRR and the cost of capital

The IRR is a *measure* of profitability that depends upon the value and timing of a project's cash flows. By contrast, the opportunity cost of capital is a *standard* of profitability. It is used to calculate the NPV of a project.

CAPITAL RATIONING

If a company had access to unlimited cash then any investment project that is expected to produce a positive net present value at the cost of capital would be accepted. However, there will be constraints such as capital expenditure budgets, which will prevent a business from undertaking all the projects it wants to. A method is required which ranks projects within the available cash resources yet gives the highest possible overall net present value. This means that projects must be selected on the basis of their present value and the initial outlay required to produce it. This is called the profitability index and is explained below.

Profitability Index (PI): Project Alpha. Cost of capital is 10%

Year	Cash inflow/(outflow) £000s	Discount factor	Present value £000s
0	(50)	1	(50)
1	100	0.91	91
2	70	0.83	58
3	60	0.75	45
NPV @ 10%			**140**

$$PI = \frac{\text{PV of the initial outlay: £50,000 + NPV at the cost of capital: £144,000}}{\text{PV of the initial outlay: £50,000}} = 3.88$$

Viable projects will have a PI greater than 1. The larger the PI, the greater the return per £ of scarce capital resources. Cash should be allocated, therefore, to projects starting with the highest profitability index then descending in rank order until cash resources are exhausted.

An alternative method of calculating the PI is to take the NPV of the project (in the case of Alpha, £144,000) and to divide it by the present value of the initial outlay, £50,000. This gives 2.88.

DISCOUNTED PAYBACK PERIOD

We mentioned that the payback period is an indicator of risk since it focuses on the exposure period before the initial cost of an investment is recovered. The discounted payback period is the more appropriate criterion since it is calculated after taking into account the time value of money. It is the period taken before the NPV of a project reaches zero. An example is given below.

Discounted Payback Period

Year	Cash inflow/ (outflow) £000s	Discount factor at a cost of capital of 10%	Present value of cash inflows/ (outflows) £000s	Cumulative present value £000s
0	(75)	1	(75)	(75)
1	25	0.91	23	(52)
2	35	0.83	29	(23)
3	30	0.75	23	–
4	40	0.68	27	27
NPV @ 10%				**27**

The discounted payback period is three years.

Summary

We have now covered the basic quantitative tools that should be used in project appraisal. They are:

- *The net present value at the cost of capital.* This is the additiona. shareholder value or the extra cash flows that will be generated by accepting a project. It ignores any cash resource constraints.
- *The internal rate of return.* This is the discount rate at which the ne present value is equal to zero. It is a measure of capital efficiency.
- *Profitability index.* This is an NPV-based measure that highlights present value per £ of investment. It is another measure of capita efficiency.
- *The discounted payback period.* This is the length of time a project takes before the net present value becomes zero. It is the break-ever time, the period of exposure before the net present value becomes positive. It is a measure of risk.

Together, these tools provide the basic economic assessment. However. they need to be set in the context of competitive and strategic factors tc demonstrate that the overall business case and not just the financial one is soundly based. For example, how will the project achieve competitive advantage? Does the project use a new technology such as a new raw material? For how long will the competitive advantage last? These are important questions that will influence the forecasting of the cash flows.

All of this indicates that sound business judgement is required. All four economic criteria need to be looked at as well as the business rationale before a final decision is made. For example, if absolute certainty is looked for, very few projects will be accepted. On the other hand, if the assumptions supporting the estimates of cash flows are too optimistic, the consequence will be an uneconomic project. The important issues that need to be taken into account in arriving at a sound business judgement are considered in the next part of the chapter.

IMPORTANT ISSUES TO CONSIDER

Incremental cash flows

We have seen already that the value and timing of cash flows only are relevant in a project appraisal. However, there are two other important points. First, cash flows should be estimated on an additional or incremental basis and, second, the consequential effects on the remainder of the business should be considered.

The incremental cash flows represent the difference between the cash flows *with* the investment and the cash flows without it. For example, if BAA, the owners of the proposed new Terminal 5 at Heathrow Airport, expected the present value of its future cash flows to be £3 billion with the investment and £2.5 billion without it, then the incremental cash flow, which should be included in the Terminal's appraisal, is £0.5 billion.

Examples of the consequential cash flow effects of a project on the rest of the business include disruption costs, such as redundancy payments and the temporary closure of premises such as retail shops while refurbishment is taking place. These consequential effects should be allowed for in the cash flow estimates.

The corollary of this is that cash flows which will not be affected by the decision to proceed with the project should be *excluded*.

Sunk costs and allocated or common costs

Sunk costs are past and irreversible cash outflows (spilt milk!). For example, BAA up to 31 March 1998 had invested £158 million in the Terminal 5 project at Heathrow. A project appraisal now of Terminal 5 should exclude the £158 million of previous expenditure. It is irrecoverable and, therefore, irrelevant. Project appraisal is concerned with future incremental cash flows. However, the lessons of the experience of spending the £158 million, such as the revised building costs, should be reflected in the estimate of future cash flows.

Allocated or common costs are not relevant either. For example, the manufacture of a new product may require a reallocation of existing factory space. A share of indirect costs (such as factory rent) may be allocated to the new product as a consequence. However, no additional cash is paid out so the reallocation of overheads is not relevant to the cash flow. However, incremental overheads such as extra electricity are relevant to the cash flow estimates and they should be included.

Opportunity costs

Opportunity costs may be relevant to an investment decision even when no cash is involved; they should be included in the appraisal. For example, suppose that a new warehouse uses land that could otherwise be sold for £3 million. Using the land involves a sacrifice – an opportunity cost – which is £3 million if the project does not proceed. The £3 million should be treated as if it were a cash outflow and be reflected in the appraisal.

Cost of capital

The capital a company uses in its investment projects is not free. Shareholders have to be provided with a return on their investment (a combination of dividends and share price appreciation). Borrowed capital such as bank loans has to be serviced with interest charges and the loans have to be repaid over an agreed period. The cost of capital can, therefore, be regarded as the return required by the providers of finance. One way to think about it is that it is an average of the cost of equity (the return required by shareholders) and the cost of debt (the interest charges on borrowings) weighted to reflect their relative proportions. For example:

Cost of debt: 10%
Cost of equity: 16%
Proportions of capital (a debt-equity ratio of 33.33%)
Equity 75%
Debt 25%
The average weighted cost of capital
= (0.75 x 0.16) + (0.25 x 0.10)
= 0.12 + 0.025
= 0.145 or 14.5%

Another way to approach the cost of capital is to recognize that investments are not equally risky. At one end of the scale, there are investments in government securities that are relatively risk free. At the other end, there are highly speculative investments, such as investments in high-tech companies. Investors in the more risky propositions will require a higher return on their investment. The cost of capital for such projects will be higher than it is for projects of lower risk.

The table below provides a summary of the costs of capital for a selection of UK companies in different industry sectors.

The cost of capital

Company	Sector	Return required by the providers of finance %
Marks & Spencer	Retail	12.2
BT	Telecommunications	10.2
Berkeley	House building	13.2
National Express	Transport	11.6

Source: *The Sunday Times*, 27 September 1998

Diversifiable and non-diversifiable risks

For the moment, assume that the only form of company finance is share-holders' equity. The cost of capital is then the cost of equity. Shareholders in companies recognize that investing in shares is more risky than investing in gilt-edged securities, and require a premium for doing so. Also, shareholders in companies that invest in relatively risky projects will want higher returns than those in companies with low risk projects. Most shareholders do not hold a single company's shares, but a portfolio of shares from a number of companies. Attached to any one share are two sorts of risk. The first is known as the *unique risk* attached to that share. The wider the spread of an investor's portfolio, the lower will be the volatility of the portfolio to the unique risk of any one share; it is a diversi-fiable risk. The other type of risk is that which cannot be avoided however much the portfolio is diversified. It is known as the *market* or non-diversi-fiable risk (R_m), and is the risk deriving from the vagaries of the economy.

The risk for which an investor will seek an appropriate return – the market risk, since he or she can avoid the unique risk by diversifying his or her portfolio – is measured by a parameter known as the *equity beta*.

Beta measures how sensitive a share is to movements in the stock market as a whole. If the share moves up by the same percentage as the market, it is said to have a beta of 1. If its price increases at twice the rate of the market, the share has a beta of 2, showing that it is more volatile or risky. If the reverse is true, and the share responds by only 1 per cent when the market moves by 2 per cent, the share has an equity beta of 0.5. The expected return from a share is connected with its beta by what is known as the security market line, as shown in Figure 12.1. Datastream (summer 1998) estimates that BAA's beta is 0.91 and Rentokil Initial's is 1.1.

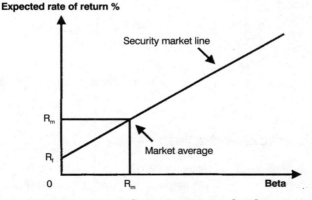

Figure 12.1 *The security market line*

The capital asset pricing model (CAPM)

This states that the cost of equity capital depends on the average premium expected by the market over the return on a risk-free investment (R_f), factored by the relative market risk of the investment (R_m).

Cost of equity capital = Risk-free return + Expected market premium × Risk factor (beta)

$CoC = R_f + (R_m - R_f) \beta$

Datastream estimates that, in the UK, for the 10 years to May 1998, R_f = 6 per cent and $Rm - R_f$ = 5.6 per cent.

In the past, it has been argued that since the interest cost of debt is usually less than the expected return on equity, an increase in the relative proportion of debt would result in a lower cost of capital. Modern thinking, as explained in the CAPM, is that the cost of capital is based on the risks inherent in the investment, and is unaffected by the way the investment is financed.

The corollary is that if the level of debt is increased, the interest cost is increased, and the remaining earnings attributable to shareholders become more volatile. The consequence is not that the cost of capital is changed, but that the cost of equity alters.

For example, in our previous illustration, the overall cost of capital was 14.5 per cent and reflected the expected return on the investment based upon its market risks. An increase in the proportion of debt to 40 per cent (from 25 per cent) would have the following effect (where E is the cost of equity; equity is now 60 per cent rather than 75 per cent of total capital):

Cost of capital = Weighted average of the costs of equity and debt

0.145	=	0.6 E	+	(0.4 x 0.10)
0.6. E	=	0.145	–	0.04
E	=	0.175	or	17.5%

The increased level of debt, moving the debt-equity ratio from 33.33 per cent to 67 per cent (40:60) has pushed up the return expected on equity to 17.5 per cent.

Sensitivity analysis and risk

Any of the four evaluation techniques (the NPV, IRR, payback period and PI) can be combined with techniques to provide more insight about the variability or riskiness of a project. Cash flows contain 'best guess' estimates, but by using sensitivity analysis the critical factors can be identified by testing the economic vulnerability of a project to changes in a particular variable. It is a 'What if?' type of approach. For example:

- How does the IRR change if sales volumes are only 75 per cent of the expected level?
- What is the effect on the IRR if the start of the project is delayed by 12 months?
- What happens to the NPV if capital costs are 15 per cent above budget?

Individual factors are varied independently, one by one, to determine how sensitive the project's viability is to changes in the key variables. The drawback to the method is that each factor is changed on the assumption that the other variables are unaltered. In practice, of course, it is likely that a change in one variable such as a delay to the start of a project may be associated with changes in other variables such as sales volume forecasts.

This approach is sometimes referred to as 'main parameter adjustment' (varying the principal assumptions supporting the cash flows and determining the effect on the NPV of the project).

An alternative approach is break-even analysis, which examines how large a change in each of the main assumptions would render the project just non-economic. This is done by increasing or decreasing the value of the cash flows for each of the assumptions until the NPV of the project at the given discount rate is zero. While making these calculations for each variable, all the other variables remain constant.

The results of such an analysis are valuable since they indicate what particular risks pose major dangers to the project and in what areas further forecasting and research efforts should be directed.

The technique of *Monte Carlo Simulation* allows the probability of forecasts varying to be quantified and examined. It requires that a range of values is estimated for each of the main project factors (rather than a single forecast estimate), together with an estimate of the probability of each of them occurring. For example, instead of a simple forecast for annual detergent sales of 35,000 units, they might be forecast as:

Sales	Probability
30,000	0.1
32,500	0.2
35,000	0.4
37,000	0.2
40,000	0.1

Note that the percentage probabilities add to 1.0.

A computer is then used to select a value for each of the project factors based on the probability of it occurring, and an IRR is calculated. The calculation is then repeated many times (perhaps several thousand). This enables a picture of the probability distribution for the project's IRR to be built up. For example, it might conclude that there is a 90 per cent probability that an IRR of 11 per cent will be exceeded, a 50 per cent probability that 15 per cent will be exceeded, and a 10 per cent chance that 2_ per cent might be reached.

Inflation

Between January 1988 and October 1998, the general level of retail prices rose at an annual average compound rate of approximately 4.4 per cent Therefore, the effects of inflation on future investment projects are likely to be significant.

There are two approaches commonly used to deal with inflation. Both recognize that the cost of capital includes an expectation for the future rate of inflation. One approach is to exclude inflation from both the cash flow predictions and the cost of capital. Cash flows are projected in 'real' terms, and a 'real' cost of capital is used. The second approach is to use the estimated cost of capital including forecast inflation. Projections are in 'money of the day' terms, and a 'money of the day' cost of capital is used. The two approaches are equivalent, and should result in the same investment decision.

Whichever method is used, it is important to realize that while general inflation can be handled by including or excluding it from both the projected flows and the cost of capital, the impact of differential inflation (prices and costs increasing at different rates) can make large differences to the NPVs and IRRs calculated. For example:

Winchester Limited

1. Forecast cash flows in 'money of the day' terms. Inflation is taken into account.
2. Convert the 'money of the day' cash flows into 'real' cash flows by applying an inflation index.
3. Apply the 'real' cost of capital to the 'real' cash flows to compute the 'real' NPV and the other indicators.

- Inflation assumption = 5% a year
- 'Real' cost of capital = 7%

	Year 0 £m	Year 1 £m	Year 2 £m	Year 3 £m
A. Capital expenditure	(100)	–	–	–
B. Cash outflows	–	(180)	(168)	–

C. Sales – cash inflows	–	263	276	23
D. Net cash flow – 'money of the day'	(100)	83	108	23
E. Inflation index	100	105	110.3	115.8
F. Net cash flow – 'real'	(100)	79	98	20
G. Discount factor at a 7% 'real' cost of capital	1	0.94	0.87	0.82
H. 'Real' present value	(100)	74	85	16
I. **Project's 'real' NPV**	**75**			

Notes:

Row D = Row C – Row B apart from Year 0 when it is Row A.
Row F = Row D ÷ Row E.
Row H = Row F × Row G.
Row I = The sum of the cash flows in Row H.

Taxation

This is a complex subject and specialist advice should be sought since practice varies from country to country. However, the principle is clear. Tax represents a cash outflow like any other business cost. It should be included in the cash flow forecasts when the tax is expected to be paid. For companies, tax is payable nine months after the year end. For example, tax on the profit for a financial year ending on 31 March will be due on the following 1 January. Corporation tax is now levied in the UK at 31 per cent of taxable profit and the rate is due to fall to 30 per cent with effect from 31 March 1999.

The depreciation charge shown in published and management accounts is not used when calculating a company's taxation liability. Instead, the Inland Revenue operates a system of capital allowances that may be set off against taxable profits. There are industrial building and plant and equipment allowances.

Capital allowances on industrial buildings are allowed at the rate of 4 per cent per year on a straight-line basis. An industrial building is defined as a structure within which a qualifying trade is carried out. Commercial offices and shops are excluded, but most factory buildings and warehouses qualify. Industrial building allowances may be claimed first for the accounting period in which the building is brought into use.

On plant and equipment, allowances are granted at 25 per cent, calculated on a reducing balance basis, and can first be claimed in the accounting period when the expenditure occurred. The reducing balance basis is illustrated below for plant and equipment bought for £100,000 in year 1.

	Opening tax value (£)	25% Capital allowance (£)	Closing tax value (£)
Year 1	100,000	25,000	75,000
Year 2	75,000	18,750	56,250

... and so on.

It should be noted that a full year's allowance can be claimed for the year in which a building is opened or a machine is bought and installed, irrespective of when in the year that event occurs.

Residual value

It may be possible to dispose of some or all of the assets used in a project when the project comes to the end of its life. If so, the estimated cash proceeds or residual value should be included in the cash flow estimates. The residual value may, however, be negative since additional costs such as decommissioning may be required to dispose of the assets. North Sea oil rigs are an example.

Terminal value

The NPV of a project is based on the cash flow projections for an estimated number of years. This is referred to as the 'time horizon'. For some projects, however, such as property developments, the cash flows will stabilize and continue beyond the time horizon but it is not realistic to forecast them indefinitely year by year. This means that a terminal value should be calculated as explained in the example below.

Alpha Limited

Alpha Limited proposes to proceed with a property development based on the following cash flow projections. Its cost of capital is 10 per cent. The company expects cash flow to stabilize after year 8 and to grow at 2 per cent annually thereafter.

Year	Net cash flow £m	Discount factor at 10%	Present value of cash flow £m
0	−20.00	1	−20.00
1	5.00	0.91	4.55
2	6.00	0.83	4.98
3	7.20	0.75	5.40
4	8.64	0.68	5.88
5	9.50	0.62	5.89
6	10.45	0.56	5.85
7	11.50	0.51	5.87
8	12.07	0.47	5.67
NPV			**24.09**

The terminal value of the cash flows after year 8 is given by the formula:

$$\frac{1}{(1.1)^2} \times \frac{12.07}{(0.10 - 0.02)} = £125.22 \text{ million}$$

Thus, the total NPV of the project is £24.09 million plus £125.22 million to give £149.31 million.

Foreign exchange

Investment opportunities are evaluated by comparing forecast outflows of cash with subsequent inflows. When the flows are all in one currency, it is clear that we are comparing like with like. However, when the flows are in different currencies, the comparison of like with like is more difficult, and will be affected by exchange rate variations.

A company investing in a subsidiary in a country other than its own must recognize that the cash flows the subsidiary generates will be different from the cash flows received by the parent, for two main reasons. The first is that there may be exchange controls in the subsidiary's country that prevent the subsidiary from remitting cash to the parent. In such a case, the parent will normally evaluate the investment based on the cash flows available to it, rather than on the cash flows available to the subsidiary. The second reason is that the exchange rate between the two currencies may vary, affecting the sterling cash flows received by the parent.

Working capital

Working capital requirements should not be forgotten in cash flow estimates. You will recall that working capital is the difference between current assets (such as stocks and trade debtors) and current liabilities (such as trade creditors). Some projects may involve an additional investment in working capital. For example, in the case of a new product, additional credit will need to be extended to customers and an additional investment will need to be made in stocks (offset by the extent to which the stocks can be financed by suppliers). At the end of the life of a project, the level of working capital will fall and may disappear altogether as stocks are liquidated, cash is received from customers and final cash payments are made to suppliers.

BUSINESS CASE PRESENTATIONS

At this stage in our discussion on investment appraisal, the basic financial indicators and the other factors that need to be considered have been discussed in some detail. The next step is to bring all this material together in the form of what is sometimes referred to as a 'business case presentation' – a formal written and verbal submission by a member of the management team asking directors or senior managers for approval to proceed with a project.

Projects submitted in a business case presentation should be derived from and be consistent with the strategy a business is pursuing. Quite apart from the calculations, the strategic rationale will need to be explained clearly since projects will only produce shareholder value if they improve the ability of a business to achieve its objectives and improve its competitive position. British Petroleum, for example, is most insistent on requiring all business cases to identify the sources of value such as the benefit of cheaper raw materials and the fixed cost savings arising from the closure of old plant and equipment.

A checklist of the points which business case presentations should include is given below:

1. Introduce and summarize the project by providing:
   background information and a clear definition of the business proposition – a description of the project and the proposed amount and nature of the capital expenditure;
   details of the economic justification such as the NPV at the cost of capital, the IRR, the discounted payback period and the profitability index;
   information about the most important assumptions and sensitivities and the principal risks involved.
2. Highlight the strategic rationale by clearly identifying the sources of value
   include references to competitor activity and assess the other project options which have been considered;
   demonstrate that the project being presented is the 'best' one;
   refer to the consequences of not proceeding with the project – the 'do nothing' option.
3. Provide comprehensive details of the engineering and technical aspects of the project and demonstrate how they will help to produce competitive advantage.
4. Produce supporting information, which:
   provides details of the estimated costs for each major part of the project and their timing;
   highlights the assumptions supporting the cash flow projections, for example, sales volumes and market shares;
   demonstrates that the lessons of experience with similar projects in the past have been learnt and are reflected in the economic justification;

provides all the detailed 'back up' for the NPV, IRR, discounted payback and profitability index calculations;
identifies the major business and technical risks which are involved and how they will be managed to mitigate their effects.

Post-project appraisal

It is most important that the lessons and experience gained from earlier projects should be applied to new investment opportunities. There is one vital question which needs to be raised: 'To what extent did past projects achieve their business and technical objectives?' The reasons for any underperformance, for example the time for building a new factory was significantly underestimated, need to be explored so that the estimates given in new projects are more realistic and can be treated with greater confidence.

SUMMARY

Capital expenditure decisions help to determine the future success or failure of a company. Therefore, it is extremely important to ensure that the appraisal process is rigorous and wide ranging so that an overall business, and not just a financial, assessment is carried out.

The time value of money is a crucial concept which means that the accounting rate of return, by itself, is an inadequate measure. Instead, the four most appropriate indicators are: the net present value (NPV) of future cash flows at the cost of capital, the IRR or internal rate of return, the discounted payback period and the profitability index. These economic criteria will then be balanced by a range of other factors such as an assessment of the risks involved before a final decision can be taken. It is a matter of commercial judgement – the 'financials' are just one aspect to consider.

As part of the financial appraisal, the following issues need to be taken into account:

- a focus on the incremental cash flows;
- the exclusion of sunk and allocated costs;
- careful thought about opportunity costs;
- confidence that the cost of capital is accurate;
- evidence that a comprehensive sensitivity analysis has been carried out;
- the effect of inflation has been properly allowed for;
- the tax effects have been calculated;

- residual and terminal values have been included;
- exchange rate fluctuations have been considered;
- working capital has been included.

And, finally, a professional 'business case' has been prepared.

Glossary of Important Finance and Accounting Terms

Note that the terms printed in italic are defined elsewhere in the glossary.

Absorption costing   A system of costing where products and services absorb a share of indirect costs such as business rates and rent, in addition to their direct costs such as labour and raw materials. A direct cost can be specifically allocated to a product or service. An indirect or overhead cost cannot be directly related to a product or service.

Accounting equation   This states that total assets are equal to total liabilities. The word 'liabilities' is sometimes used to mean amounts owed to third parties (creditors) only; in this case the equation is total assets equal total liabilities plus *equity*. See *balance sheet*.

Accounts payable   The US term for *trade creditors*.

Accounts receivable   The US term for *debtors*.

Accruals and accrued charges/accrued income   Outstanding expenses for an accounting period which have not yet been paid, and/or cash received in respect of goods and services to be provided in a future accounting period. An example of an accrued charge is unpaid income tax (PAYE). An example of accrued income is cash received in advance from customers before goods have been delivered.

Acid-test ratio   A measure of the ability of a business to meet its short-term commitments (short term means within 12 months). The ratio is calculated by dividing current assets, excluding stock, by current liabilities. Current assets are debtors (such as amounts due from customers), cash balances, and short-term investments that can be easily converted into cash. Current liabilities include amounts due to suppliers, bank overdrafts, and amounts due for unpaid expenses such as telephone bills, as well as dividends and taxes payable.

Activity-based costing   The identification of activities such as distribution and purchasing as a basis for charging indirect costs to products and services.

Amortization   A reduction in debt by periodic payments covering interest and part of the principal. The term is also used for the process of writing down intangible assets, such as a lease, over their expected commercial life.

Asset turnover   This is a ratio that measures the effectiveness with which a business uses its *assets* to generate *sales*, revenues or turnover. It is calculated by dividing sales by *capital employed*.

Assets   Everything that a company owns or that is due to it: cash, investments, cash due, materials and stocks are called *current assets*; buildings and machinery are known as *fixed assets*; patents and goodwill are called *intangible assets*.

Associated company   A company over which another has significant influence. A company will be presumed to be an associated company if ownership is between 20 and 50 per cent of the voting share capital. Above 50 per cent, the company becomes a subsidiary. Under 20 per cent ownership, the holding becomes a trade investment.

Balance sheet   A statement of the financial position of a business at a particular date showing the various categories of *assets* and how they have been financed. Assets are financed by *liabilities*.

Bond (or note)   A written promise to pay the holder a sum of money at a certain time (usually more than one year after issue) at a stated rate of interest. It is a long-term financial obligation.

Book value   The value of an *asset* as recorded in the financial statements. For a fixed asset it will be the original cost (unless amended by *revaluation*) less the *depreciation* that has so far been accumulated on it. This may be called the net book value or written down value. The book value of an *ordinary share* is the sum of the ordinary *share capital* and *reserves*, the *equity*, divided by the number of issued shares.

Break-even point   The level of output or revenues, sales or turnover at which total revenues equal total costs.

Budgetary control   Short-term financial planning to meet objectives in the financial year against which actual results will then be compared.

Capital allowances   The Inland Revenue's equivalent of a company's depreciation charge, which is not allowable for tax purposes. Allowances are granted on the purchase of certain *fixed assets* such as plant and machinery and industrial buildings. They have the effect of reducing taxable profit.

Capital employed   This is a term for which there are a variety of definitions. A common one is: total *assets* (*fixed assets* plus current assets) less *current liabilities*, which is the same as fixed assets plus *working capital*. This is equal to the long-term finance invested in the business in the form of long-term *liabilities*, *debt* and *equity*.

A similar phrase is 'net operating assets' or 'net trading assets' which excludes financial assets such as cash and monetary liabilities such as bank borrowings.

Capital expenditure   Expenditure on *fixed assets* such as plant and equipment. Except for freehold land, the cost is spread over several financial periods through the process of *depreciation*. The value of the fixed assets (less the depreciation accumulated to date) is capitalized – shown in the *balance sheet*. The depreciation charged each year is an *operating cost* in the *profit and loss account* or income statement.

Net capital expenditure is capital expenditure less the proceeds from *asset* disposals such as those arising from the sale of fixed assets.

Capital gearing or **gearing**   The proportion of borrowings in relation to *equity* shareholders' funds. It is commonly measured by the *debt to equity ratio*. For this purpose, *debt* is normally defined as total borrowings or interest-bearing obligations including leases, less cash balances and short-term investments such as cash deposits.

In US terminology, gearing is known as 'financial leverage'.

Capitalization or **market capitalization**   The value of a company based on the market price of its shares; it is, therefore, equal to the number of shares issued times their market price summed for all the types of shares issued.

Market capitalization is used sometimes to include the market value of all the company's traded securities, including *bonds* and *debentures*.

Cash flow   The generation of cash by a business. 'Operating' cash flow is equal to operating profit plus amounts that do not reflect cash movements (such as *depreciation*) less the increase in *working capital*. 'Free' cash flow is the operating cash flow less *capital expenditure*, financing charges and *corporation tax* payments. This cash flow is 'free' in the sense that it is available to meet cash dividend payments to ordinary shareholders.

For a business unit or subsidiary, which is part of a group of companies, cash flow is defined sometimes as operating cash flow less capital expenditure. This is a measure of the extent to which the business unit is self-sufficient in cash terms.

Cash flow statement   A statement which explains the impact of operating, investment and financial transactions on a company's cash position between two *balance sheet* dates.

Collection period or **days sales outstanding**   The average length of time taken by a customer to pay a sales invoice. It is calculated by dividing *trade debtors* by annual *sales,* times 365 days to give the average number of days for which the sales invoice has been outstanding.

Commercial paper   Unsecured short-term borrowings normally for a maximum of one year.

Common stock   The US term for 'ordinary shares'.

Contingent liability   A liability that is contingent upon the occurrence or non-occurrence of one or more uncertain future events, for example unresolved legal disputes.

Contribution   The difference between *sales* and direct or *variable costs* before charging indirect or *fixed costs.*

Convertible   A bond, debenture, or *preferred share* that may be exchanged by the owner for ordinary *shares* in accordance with the terms of the issue.

Corporation tax   The tax levied on a company's taxable profit. Taxable profit is not the same as the 'profit before taxation' in the profit and loss account because various items are allowable and disallowable for tax purposes. Examples of allowable items are capital allowances (the taxation equivalent of depreciation to encourage capital expenditure) and specific provisions for bad debts. Examples of disallowable items are depreciation, staff entertainment and general provisions for bad debts.

The current corporation tax rate is 31 per cent of taxable profit. The rate is due to fall to 30 per cent in April 1999. A small company rate applies to those companies with insufficient profit to be taxed at the higher rate.

Cost   The charge against profits made for the use or consumption of resources during an accounting period. It is not necessarily the same as the cash actually spent in the period in view of adjustments for *depreciation, accruals* and *provisions.* See *operating cost.*

Cost centre A physical location within an organization such as a department or section where *costs* are accumulated.

Cost code A numbering system used to describe the type, source and purpose of all *costs* and *revenues*.

Cost of capital This is the return required by the providers of finance – lenders and shareholders – which reflects the risks they face. The weighted average cost of capital is the required rate of return reflecting the relative proportions of finance provided by lenders and shareholders.

Cost of sales or **cost of goods sold** This is the direct cost to the business of the products or services sold to its customers.

Cost of sales adjustment or **COSA** The excess of the replacement cost or current cost of goods sold over their historical cost. It is a term used in inflation accounting (*current cost accounting*) or in replacement cost accounting.

Cost unit Any product or service to which *costs* can be charged.

Creditors Any person or organization to whom a company has a commitment apart from shareholders (the owners). For example, *trade creditors* are suppliers of goods for whom unpaid bills are outstanding. It is a legal requirement to distinguish between short-term creditors (due to be paid within 12 months of the balance sheet date), called *current liabilities*, and long-term creditors (amounts due to be paid after one year). A typical example of a long-term creditor is a bank that has supplied a loan. Short and long-term borrowings are disclosed separately.

Current assets Assets such as *debtors* and *stocks*, which can be converted into cash within 12 months of the balance sheet date. Cash balances and short-term investments (such as stock market investments) are also part of current assets. They are sometimes referred to as *liquid resources*.

Current cost accounting A system of accounting, intended to measure the impact of changing prices, which is based on replacement cost.

Current liabilities Short-term liabilities that have to be paid within 12 months of the balance sheet date. Examples are *trade creditors*, bank overdrafts (repayable on demand) and *accrued charges*.

Current ratio The ratio of *current assets* divided by *current liabilities*. It is a broad measure of the ability of a business to meet its short-term commitments. The *acid-test ratio*, however, is a more sensitive measure. It is the trend in the current ratio which needs to be monitored carefully, especially the extent to which current liabilities are rising faster than current assets.

Debentures A form of long-term borrowing which may be secured by a mortgage or charge on a specific asset such as a property. A stated rate of interest (which may be variable) is paid. Normally, it has a fixed repayment date (or range of repayment dates). Debentures may be traded on the Stock Exchange. See *bond*.

Debt Interest-bearing liabilities such as short- and long-term bank loans.

Debt-equity ratio The relationship of interest-bearing borrowings, including lease obligations, to *equity* shareholders' funds. It is also known as the *gearing* or *leverage* ratio. A common definition is net borrowings (total borrowings less short-term deposits and cash balances) expressed as a percentage of equity shareholders' funds.

Debtors Amounts due from third parties. The largest element is usually *trade debtors* – amounts due from customers. The US term is 'accounts receivable'.

Deferred taxation This is caused by the timing differences that arise when a transaction is recognized for accounting purposes and when it is recognized for *corporation tax* purposes. One of the main sources is the difference in the timing of *depreciation* and the permitted allowances claimed against taxable profits. These tax allowances are called *capital allowances*.

Depreciation A charge or cost in the profit and loss account to write off the cost, less any salvage value, of a *fixed asset* over its estimated useful life. It is a bookkeeping entry and does not represent any cash outlay.

Differential or **incremental costs and revenues** The costs and/or revenues of different options which are compared to identify the differences between them.

Discounted cash flow (DCF) A method used to calculate the present value of cash flows taking into account the time value of money.

Dividend The payment recommended by the board of directors and approved by the shareholders to be distributed pro rata among the shares outstanding. On *preferred shares*, it is generally a fixed amount. On *ordinary shares*, the dividend varies with the fortunes of the company and the amount of cash available. It may be omitted, at the discretion of the directors, if performance is poor or they decide to retain cash to finance acquisitions and invest in plant and equipment. Sometimes a company will pay a dividend based on past earnings even if it is not operating at a profit; the dividend is then said to be 'uncovered'.

Dividend cover   The profit attributable to the ordinary shareholders – the *earnings* – divided by the total *dividend*; it is a measure of the security of the dividend payment. The higher the dividend cover, the more secure the dividend since, if earnings fall, the less likely it will be that the dividend will be reduced. An uncovered dividend will have a dividend cover of less than one. Such a situation may lead to future dividends being reduced or 'passed' (no dividend at all).

Dividend yield   The annual *dividend* per share expressed as a percentage of the share price. A relatively low dividend yield implies that an investor is prepared to accept a low dividend income today. The expectation is that the share price will rise since the earnings prospects of the company are perceived to be good. The expectation of an appreciation in the share price is compensation for the relatively low dividend income.

A relatively high dividend yield implies that an investor is not prepared to wait for an appreciation in the share price because the outlook for earnings growth is perceived to be poor and/or the risk of holding the company's shares is perceived to be high. In both cases, an investor wants a relatively high dividend income as compensation for the uncertain future prospects. A variation on dividend cover is the payout ratio, which is the annual dividend expressed as a percentage of earnings. For example, a dividend cover of two is equivalent to a payout ratio of 50 per cent.

Double entry bookkeeping   The method of recording financial transactions whereby every item is entered as a debit or credit in one account and a corresponding credit or debit in another.

Earnings   The profit after taxation and all other charges less preference *dividends* and the minority interest and after *exceptional* and *extraordinary items*. It is the profit attributable to the ordinary shareholders – the 'bottom line'. The US expression for earnings is 'net income'.

Earnings per share (EPS)   The *earnings* divided by the number of issued ordinary shares. Growth in EPS is an important financial performance indicator.

Earnings yield   The *earnings* per share expressed as a percentage of the market price of an ordinary share. The reciprocal of the earnings yield is the *price/earnings ratio (P/E ratio)*.

Equity   The ownership interest of ordinary shareholders in a company. It is referred to also as net assets, net worth, share capital and reserves, shareholders' funds, the shareholders' interest, or equity shareholders' funds.

Exceptional items   See *extraordinary items*.

Expenditure   See *capital expenditure* and *revenue expenditure*.

Extraordinary items   Items that are both abnormal in size and in nature and are not expected to occur frequently or regularly, such as the expropriation of assets held abroad. There are also exceptional costs which are abnormal in size but not in nature, such as large provisions for bad debts and significant redundancy costs. With the introduction of Financial Reporting Standard Number 3 in October 1992, virtually all extraordinary items are now treated as exceptional.

Factoring/invoice discounting   The receipt of cash from a specialist factoring company. This is arranged against the security of approved sales invoices for a fee. The specialist company collects the cash later from customers.

Fair value   A concept close to *replacement cost*. It is used for the 'arms length' asset valuation of an acquisition; it is important in determining *goodwill*.

FIFO (first-in first-out)   A method of stock valuation based on the assumption that the items remaining in stock are those that were purchased most recently.

Fixed assets   Assets such as property, plant and equipment, which have been purchased to provide the basis for a company's long-term future. They are expected to be used for more than a year.

Fixed cost   A cost that stays the same for a period over a specified range of output levels, for example, the basic salaries of the sales force.

Flexible budget   A budget that changes according to the actual level of activity or output achieved.

Gearing   See *capital gearing*.

Goodwill   The excess paid by an acquiring company over the *book value* or *fair value* of the net *assets* of another company. Goodwill is an example of an intangible asset. It is amortized over its estimated useful life – up to 20 years.

Gross profit and **gross profit margin**   The difference between *sales* and the *cost of sales*. Gross profit margin is gross profit divided by sales expressed as a percentage. It is a vitally important indicator for most businesses because it measures both the profitability and the relative profitability of a company's products.

Group accounts   The accounts of the *holding company* and its *subsidiaries*.

Historical cost   This is the traditional way of valuing *assets* in a *balance sheet* and costs in the *profit and loss account* or income statement. The criterion for valuation is the cost incurred at the time of purchase, the acquisition cost. This system of accounting is known as 'historical cost accounting' (HCA), or as 'accounting in accordance with the historical cost convention'. Some financial statements are prepared under the historical cost convention modified by the revaluation of certain assets, usually property, to their current value.

Holding company   The parent company that owns a controlling interest in one or more subsidiaries.

Income   The US term for 'profit'. Net income is usually the equivalent of profit after tax (*earnings*).

Income statement   See *profit and loss account*.

Intangible assets   Items of value to a company which do not have a physical shape; examples are patents and trademarks. *Goodwill* may also be included.

Interest cover   An indicator of *solvency*: it is calculated by expressing profit before interest and taxation (the *operating* or *trading profit*) as a multiple of the interest charge. It is a measure of the ability of a business to service its financing costs from the profit it earns from its trading activities.

Internal rate of return (IRR)   The rate of return or discount rate used in the appraisal of a project which produces a net present value of cash flows equal to zero. It is a measure of a project's profitability.

Inventory   The US word for *stocks*.

Lease   The hire of a fixed asset such as plant and machinery from a leasing company – the lessor. There are two sorts of leases. An operating lease is a short-term contract. At the end of the period, the *asset* concerned is returned to the lessor and the leasing charges are charged to the *profit and loss account* for the appropriate period. A finance lease is a long-term contract. The value of the leased asset is shown or 'capitalized' in the *balance sheet* (unlike an operating lease).

The commitment to the lessor is split between short- and long-term creditors. The asset concerned is depreciated each year by the amount of the capital repayments. Interest charges on the lease agreement are charged to the profit and loss account when they are incurred.

Liability   Amounts owed by the business. Its usage varies: 'total liabilities' can mean *equity* or shareholders' interest plus amounts due to *creditors,* but it may be used to mean amounts owed to third parties or creditors only such as banks and suppliers.

LIFO (last-in first-out)   A method of *stock* valuation that assumes that the last item delivered to stock is the first to be used. The cost charged in the *profit and loss account* is, therefore, the most recent cost and, in times of inflation, will be higher than under *FIFO*. It is not accepted as a method by the Inland Revenue, but it is sometimes used in management accounts to maintain up-to-date costs.

Liquid resources   Cash and bank balances plus short-term investments that can be easily converted into cash, such as money market deposits.

Liquidity   A measure of the ability of a business to meet its short-term commitments. If expansion is too rapid, *trade debtors* and *stocks* may increase to such an extent that *creditors* cannot be paid reasonably promptly because cash flow is inadequate. This is called over-trading. See also the *acid-test ratio* and the *current ratio*.

Marginal costing   A system of costing used for decision-making purposes which focuses on the recovery of direct, incremental or *variable costs* only – to be used with caution.

Minority interest   Many subsidiary companies are not fully owned by the parent company (although the parent company will own more than 50 per cent). Such companies are partly owned by *minority* shareholders – shareholders who hold shares in the *subsidiary*.
   In the preparation of consolidated or group financial statements, all the *assets*, expenses, *liabilities* and *revenues* of subsidiaries are included in the group accounts. This is because the group fully controls the subsidiary, even if it does not fully own it. In such financial statements, the subsidiary is amalgamated into the rest of the group, and the capital provided by the minority shareholders is separately recognized as a part of the capital of the group called 'minority interest'. This amount grows each time the relevant subsidiary makes a profit that is not fully distributed. In the consolidated *profit and loss account*, the share of the subsidiary's profit owned by minorities is also shown, as 'profit attributable to minorities', or as a deduction from group profit before arriving at the

profit attributable to group shareholders. The profit attributable to group shareholders is referred to as *earnings*.

Net assets   Total *assets* less all *creditors*. It is therefore equal to *equity*. Revisions of asset value from *book value* to *realizable value*, say, during a re-appraisal of a company's prospects will increase or reduce net assets, and net asset value.

Net current assets   See *working capital*.

Net present value   The sum of all the negative and positive present values of future cash flows in an investment appraisal. The present values are calculated by discounting the cash flows at the *cost of capital*. The NPV at the cost of capital is equivalent to the shareholder value created by the investment project.

Net realizable value   The value that could be obtained by disposing of *assets*. It is not normally used in financial statements, except in the valuation of *stocks*. If the realizable value is less than cost, then net realizable value should be the basis of stock valuation. In the UK, property companies revalue their property investments to market or realizable value.

Net worth   Synonymous with *net assets*, and therefore with *equity*.

Nominal value   The face value of a security. In the case of a share, it is also known as the 'par value', and may reflect the price at which shares were originally issued. However, a new share issued later may be issued at a price well above the nominal value (see *share premium*). The nominal value normally has no significance for the market value at which a share is traded.

Notes payable   The US term for 'short-term borrowings'.

Operating costs or **operating expenses**   All costs excluding interest charges and taxation. They represent those costs most directly under the control of line or operating management. Turnover or sales less operating costs equals operating or trading profit. The abbreviation, PBIT, which stands for profit before interest and taxation, is the same as operating profit.

Ordinary shares   Usually the most significant element of the share capital of a company. There may also be *preference* shares; there can be different classes of ordinary shares. The US term for ordinary shares is 'common stock'. See *earnings*.

Over-trading   See *liquidity*.

Overdraft   Cash owed on a bank current account. A form of short-term borrowing. It is repayable on demand.

Paid-in surplus   The US phrase for *share premium*.

Par value   See *nominal value*.

Payback period   (Strictly speaking the discounted payback period.) The length of time before the present value of the cumulative cash flows reaches zero. This is equivalent to the length of time before a project recovers the present value of the initial cash outflows. It is the 'break-even' time and is a measure of capital efficiency and risk.

Preferred shares   *Dividends* on preferred shares must be paid before dividends may be paid on *ordinary shares*, hence the word 'preferred'. They are paid at a set percentage of the *nominal value* of the preferred shares. For cumulative preferred shares, all past unpaid preference dividends must be paid before an ordinary share dividend is paid. Preferred shares are not part of a company's *equity*.

Pre-payment   A cash payment which includes an element covering a future accounting period. An example is rent paid in advance.

Present value   The equivalent value today of cash receivable at some time in the future. It is calculated by multiplying future cash flows by discount factors that depend on when the cash is expected to be received.

Price-earnings ratio (P/E ratio)   The market price of a share divided by the *earnings* per share to give the number of years' earnings represented by the current share price. It is a financial status symbol. The higher the P/E ratio, the more attractive a company's *earnings* prospects are perceived to be. The historic P/E ratio is based on the latest reported earnings per share. The forward or prospective P/E ratio is based on the forecast earnings per share.

Profit   The difference between the *sales* generated and the *costs* incurred for an accounting period. In view of the 'matching' principle, it is not the same as cash received since sales are recognized when goods or services are supplied (rather than when they are paid for by the customer). Costs are incurred during the time period to which they relate (rather than when they are paid in cash).

Profit after taxation (earnings)   The *profit* after all *costs*, including financing costs or interest charges and taxation, but before *dividends*. See *earnings*.

Profit and loss account or **income statement**   A summary of the *sales*, revenue or turnover generated less the *costs* incurred for an accounting period. The profit and loss account is concerned with financial performance during a given time period. See *profit*. By contrast, the *balance sheet* is concerned with financial position at a particular date.

Profit before taxation   The *profit* after all *costs*, including financing costs or interest charges, but before taxation and dividends.

Profit margin   A measure of the profitability of *sales*. It is defined as the profit before or after interest and taxation expressed as a percentage of sales. The operating or trading margin is the profit before interest and taxation expressed as a percentage of sales.

Profitability index   The *net present value* of future cash flows is divided by the *present value* of future cash outflows or cash outlays. It is a measure of capital efficiency, which ranks projects according to the net present value they generate per £ of investment. The profitability index can also be defined as the present value of future cash inflows divided by the present value of future cash outflows. Project rankings are unchanged regardless of which definition is used. The profitability index is used when the cash available for capital expenditure is limited. This situation is referred to as 'capital rationing'.

Provision   An additional allowance for a cost or charge incurred but not paid at the *balance sheet* date. Examples of provisions are the estimated cost of redundancies and the costs of reorganizing a business. Provisions may be *exceptional items* if they are significant. A provision is included as a cost in the *profit and loss account* and a liability in the balance sheet. See *accruals* and *accrued charges*. A distinction is drawn sometimes between an accrued charge (the precise amount is known) and a provision (an estimate).

Realizable asset value   The price at which an *asset*, a group of assets or a business could be sold.

Replacement cost   The cost of replacing an *asset* used as the basis for *depreciation* in *current cost accounting*.

Replacement cost or **current cost**   *Assets* may be valued at their replacement cost rather than their *historic cost*. This is sometimes done in management accounts so that a business is charged with current rather than historic levels of cost. It is the basis of *current cost accounting*.

Replacement cost operating profit   The *profit* after allowing for the extra or reduced cost of replacing *stocks* and before interest and taxation. It is used, particularly by oil companies, as an important measure of profit since *historic cost* operating profit is affected by the impact of changes in the input price of crude oil.

Reserves   Realized and unrealized gains that have added value to the business, and which form part of the *equity*. Realized gains produce *profit*; unrealized gains arise from revaluations of *assets*. A third form of gain is the *share premium* paid over and above the *nominal* or *par value* of issued new shares.

Retained profit or **retained earnings**   The profit for the year after all charges and the distribution of dividends to shareholders. The figure for retained profit in the *balance sheet* will be the accumulated retained profit since the business started to trade. It may be known as the revenue reserve or *reserves*, the profit and loss account reserve, retained earning or retained profit.

Return on capital employed (ROCE)   *Operating* or *trading profit* expressed as a percentage of *capital employed*. It is the most important measure of profitability.

Return on equity   Profit after taxation or *earnings* divided by the *equity* expressed as a percentage.

Revenue   See *sales*.

Revenue expenditure   Expenditure charged to the *profit and loss account* or income statement in the year in which it is incurred. It is not capitalized as an *asset* in the *balance sheet*. See *capital expenditure*.

Revenue reserve   See *retained profit*.

Rights issue   The sale of additional shares by a company to its existing shareholders (in proportion to their existing holdings) normally at a discount to the prevailing stock market price in order to ensure a successful issue.

Sales   The invoiced value of the goods and services provided to customers during the accounting period. It is also called revenue or turnover. It excludes VAT.

Scrip issue   A free or bonus issues of new shares to existing shareholders in proportion to their current holding. No new share capital is received and no cash is raised. A company simply converts some or all of its *retained profit* into *share capital*. Since the number of *ordinary shares* will increase, the share price will fall pro rata.

Secured loan   A loan against which a certain *asset* or assets has or have been pledged. If the company with the loan falls into default, the lender will obtain the available proceeds from the sale of these assets before any unsecured *creditors* such as suppliers.

Sensitivity analysis   A technique used in investment appraisal. It assesses the effects on the *net present value*, the *internal rate of return*, the discounted payback period and the profitability index of changes in the assumptions supporting the estimated future cash flows. Sensitivity analysis asks the 'What if?' question.

Share buy-backs   The purchase of shares by a company from its own shareholders. It has the effect of increasing earnings per share and can boost the share price.

Share capital   The permanent capital contributed directly by the owners of a business (the shareholders) both at the start of trading and, subsequently, when additional capital is required to finance expansion. Issued share capital is the amount of capital contributed by shareholders and received by the company. Authorized capital is the total amount of share capital which the directors are empowered to issue.

Share dividend   A *dividend* paid in the form of extra shares rather than in cash.

Share premium   The difference between the issue price and the *nominal* or *par value* of a share. When a premium is paid for new shares, a share premium *reserve* is created or increased.

Shareholder return   The total wealth returned to a shareholder by a company over a specific period of time. It is calculated by adding the appreciation (or fall) in the share price to the *dividend* per share received and expressing the result as a percentage of the opening share price. For example, the share price was 100p on 1 January 1998 and 110p on 31 December 1998. The dividend per share received during the year was 5p. The total gain was, therefore, 110p less 100p plus 5p to give 15p which, expressed as a percentage of the opening share price (100p), is 15 per cent. Fifteen per cent is the annual rate of shareholder return.

Shareholders' interest or shareholders' funds   The sum of *share capital* plus *share premium* plus *retained profit* plus other *reserves*, at the *balance sheet* date. Synonymous with *equity, net worth* and *net assets*.

Solvency   The ability of a business to meet its long-term commitments. See also *debt-equity ratio* and *interest cover*.

Standard costing   A system of costing – predetermined costs are compared with actual costs to highlight variances which are then investigated.

Stock turnover rate   The average number of times each year that *stocks* are 'turned over' in the course of trading activity. It is calculated by dividing the *cost of sales* by average or closing stocks. (When computing the ratio from published accounts, the cost of sales may not be known; in such cases, the sales figure is normally substituted.)

Stocks   The investment a company makes in raw materials, work in progress, finished goods and supplies. They are normally valued at cost or net *realizable value*, whichever is less. The US term is 'inventory'.

Subsidiary company   See *associated company*.

Trade creditors   Amounts due to suppliers for goods and services received but not yet paid for. They are normally due for payment within 12 months of the *balance sheet* date, and are part of *current liabilities*. A capital creditor refers to unpaid amounts for *capital* rather than *revenue* expenditure, for example, unpaid bills for new plant and machinery.

Trade debtors   The amount due from customers in respect of goods and services supplied but not yet paid for. Usually reported as *current assets*, but a note may disclose that some trade debtors are not expected to pay within the coming year.

Trading or **operating profit**   *Profit* after all charges except interest, taxation, and *exceptional* and *extraordinary* items.

Trial balance   A list of debit and credit balances in individual accounts from which a *profit and loss account* and a *balance sheet* are prepared.

Variable cost   A cost that varies according to the volume of production, for example, raw material costs.

Variance   The difference between a budgeted or standard figure and the actual result.

Working capital (or net current assets)   Current assets (such as trade *debtors*, cash and *stocks*) less current liabilities (such as *trade creditors* and *accrued charges*). Trading working capital is working capital but it excludes items of a financing nature such as cash balances, bank overdrafts, proposed *dividends* and taxation. Working capital is the net investment in short-term assets which give a company the capacity or resources to trade on a day-to-day basis.

Zero-based budget   A budget compiled without reference to the previous year's budget. It challenges the status quo.

Double-entry Bookkeeping

INTRODUCTION

The principles of double-entry bookkeeping provide a number of useful explanations such as:

- where the details come from to enable financial statements to be prepared (what the sources of information are); and
- why a balance sheet balances.

Double-entry bookkeeping is a system that records both cash and credit transactions when they arise. The term 'double-entry' is derived from the procedure whereby each and every accounting transaction is entered in the 'books' twice. Two aspects of the same transaction are recognized. They are referred to as *debits* and *credits*.

When transactions were recorded in ledgers, the left side was the 'debit' side and the right side was the 'credit' side. The debit side covered assets, costs and receipts. The credit side covered liabilities, sales and payments. For example, cash received was debited and cash payments were credited. To summarize:

Debit side	Credit side
Expenses (costs)	Revenue, sales or turnover
Assets	Liabilities
Cash receipts	Cash payments

Sometimes there is confusion when our bank statement shows that we are 'in credit'. This means that we have a positive cash balance. From our point of view, the cash is an asset – a debit balance. However, from the bank's point of view, the cash is owed to us. It is a liability and a credit balance in the bank's 'books'. Similarly, trade creditors in a customer's 'books' are trade debtors in its suppliers' 'books' and vice versa.

Accounts are opened in a ledger for each type of asset, liability, revenue and cost. They are listed in a chart of accounts and identified by a code. Visualize an account as a letter 'T', with the name of the account on the crossbar and entries of figures on the left or right side of the vertical bar. In a double-entry system, each transaction is entered twice, once in two separate accounts. One entry will be on the debit (left) side of the first account. The other entry will be on the credit (right) side of the second account. Here are some examples.

Paid £200 wages on 2 March 1999 with cash drawn from the bank account.

Wages Account (£)

2.3.99   Bank   200

Bank Account (£)

2.3.99   Wages   200

Wages are an expense so the entry goes on the debit side of the wages account. The cash paid out is a credit entry in the bank account. Notice that both accounts are cross-referenced to the other.

Purchased £900 of raw materials on credit from A Supplier on 5 March 1999.

Purchases Account (£)

5.3.99   A Supplier   900

A Supplier Account (£)

5.3.99   Purchases   900

The two accounts involved are Purchases (an expense) and A Supplier (a liability). Every supplier and every customer will have his or her own separate accounts. This means that the amounts due to and due from each supplier and customer can be monitored individually.

Paid A Supplier £600 on 29 March 1999.

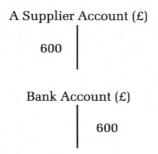

A Supplier Account (£)

600

Bank Account (£)

600

The cash payment of £600 goes on the credit side of the bank account. The other entry is a £600 debit to the A Supplier account. This means that A Supplier is still owed £300 (£900 less £600).

THE TRIAL BALANCE

At the end of an accounting period, usually the end of the month, each account is closed and all the balances are listed in a trial balance. For example, in the case of wages, there may be a number of entries on the debit side during the month. The balance on the account is the total of all those debit entries. In the case of A Supplier, there are entries on both sides of the same account. In this case, the balance is the amount by which the greater side exceeds the smaller side. For example:

A Supplier Account (£)

29.3.99 Bank	600	5.3.99 Purchases	900
Balance c/d	300		
	900		900
		1.4.99 Balance b/f	300

The credit balance carried down at the end of March and brought forward at the beginning of April is £300.

All accounts are 'balanced off' in this way. Those with either a credit o:
a debit balance are then listed in the trial balance as follows:

	Debit (£)	Credit (£)
Purchases	900	
Wages	200	
Bank		800
A Supplier		300
	£1,100	£1,100

The trial balance must always balance because identical amounts have
been entered on opposite sides in two different accounts. Therefore, it
goes some way to proving the accuracy of the recording. But it does not
prove that amounts were entered in the correct account, or that a transaction had been omitted.

The 'T' accounts are not seen as such in computerized accounting but
the basic principle of debit and credit is still observed.

The preparation of a trial balance is an essential step in the preparation
of a profit and loss account and a balance sheet, as shown below in a new
example.

St Alfred's Limited, Market Traders

Trial balance as at 30 April 1999

	Debit (£)	Credit (£)
Cash	400	
Purchases	4,000	
Wages	1,300	
Rent	1,000	
Equipment	1,500	
A Customer	700	
Share capital		500
B Supplier		200
Revenues		8,200
	£8,900	£8,900

Profit and loss account for the four months ended 30 April 1999

	(£)
Revenues	8,200
Expenses:	
Purchases	(4,000)
Wages	(1,300)
Rent	(1,000)
	(6,300)
Profit for the period	£1,900

Balance sheet as at 30 April 1999

Assets	£
Equipment	1,500
Trade debtor	700
Cash	400
	£2,600
Liabilities	
Share capital	500
Retained profit	1,900
Shareholders' interest (equity)	2,400
Trade creditor	200
	£2,600

Present Value Table

Years	3%	4%	5%	6%	7%	8%	10%	12%	14%	16%	18%	20%
1	0.971	0.962	0.952	0.943	0.935	0.926	0.909	0.893	0.877	0.862	0.847	0.833
2	0.943	0.925	0.907	0.890	0.873	0.857	0.826	0.797	0.769	0.743	0.718	0.694
3	0.915	0.889	0.864	0.840	0.816	0.794	0.751	0.712	0.675	0.641	0.609	0.579
4	0.888	0.855	0.823	0.792	0.763	0.735	0.683	0.636	0.592	0.552	0.516	0.482
5	0.863	0.822	0.784	0.747	0.713	0.681	0.621	0.567	0.519	0.476	0.437	0.402
6	0.837	0.790	0.746	0.705	0.666	0.630	0.564	0.507	0.456	0.410	0.370	0.335
7	0.813	0.760	0.711	0.665	0.623	0.583	0.513	0.452	0.400	0.354	0.314	0.279
8	0.789	0.731	0.677	0.627	0.582	0.540	0.467	0.404	0.351	0.305	0.266	0.233
9	0.766	0.703	0.645	0.592	0.544	0.500	0.424	0.361	0.308	0.263	0.225	0.194
10	0.744	0.676	0.614	0.558	0.508	0.463	0.386	0.322	0.270	0.227	0.191	0.162
11	0.722	0.650	0.585	0.527	0.475	0.429	0.350	0.287	0.237	0.195	0.162	0.135
12	0.701	0.625	0.557	0.497	0.444	0.397	0.319	0.257	0.208	0.168	0.137	0.112
13	0.681	0.601	0.530	0.469	0.415	0.368	0.290	0.229	0.182	0.145	0.116	0.093
14	0.661	0.577	0.505	0.442	0.388	0.340	0.263	0.205	0.160	0.125	0.099	0.078
15	0.642	0.555	0.481	0.417	0.362	0.315	0.239	0.183	0.140	0.108	0.084	0.065
16	0.623	0.534	0.458	0.394	0.399	0.292	0.218	0.163	0.123	0.093	0.071	0.054
17	0.605	0.513	0.436	0.371	0.317	0.270	0.198	0.146	0.108	0.080	0.060	0.045
18	0.587	0.494	0.416	0.350	0.296	0.250	0.180	0.130	0.095	0.069	0.051	0.038
19	0.570	0.475	0.386	0.331	0.277	0.232	0.164	0.116	0.083	0.060	0.043	0.031
20	0.554	0.456	0.377	0.312	0.258	0.215	0.149	0.104	0.073	0.051	0.037	0.026

Reference

Accounting Standards Committee (1988) Stocks and work in progress, *Standard Statements of Accounting Practice*, no 9, Accounting Standards Committee, London

Further Reading

Brealey, R A and Myers, S C (1996) *Principles of Corporate Finance*, 5th edn, McGraw-Hill, Maidenhead

Brett, M (1995) *How to Read the Financial Pages*, 4th edn, Century Business, London

Coopers and Lybrand (1998) *A Guide to UK Accounting Law and Practice*, Accountancy Books, London

Drury, C (1996) *Management and Cost Accounting*, 4th edn, Thomson Business Press, London

Holmes, G and Sugden, A (1997) *Interpreting Company Reports and Accounts*, 6th edn, Prentice Hall, Hemel Hempstead

Horngren, C T, Sundem, G L and Stratton, W O (1999) *Introduction to Management Accounting*, 11th edn, Prentice Hall, Englewood Cliffs, NJ

Livingstone, J L (1997) *The Portable MBA in Finance and Accounting*, 2nd edn, Wiley, Chichester

Reid, W and Myddleton, D R (1996) *The Meaning of Company Accounts*, 6th edn, Gower, Aldershot

Rice, A (1997) *Accounts Demystified*, FT Pitman, London

Sharpe, P and Keelin, T (1998) 'How SmithKline Beecham makes better resource allocation decisions,' *Harvard Business Review*, March–April

The publications of the Accounting Standards Board (01908 230344) and the International Accounting Standards Committee (0171 427 5927)

Index